M000216882

# THE SUGAR BOOK

# THE SUGAR BOOK

## Johannes Göransson

Tarpaulin Sky Press
Grafton, Vermont
2015

The Sugar Book
© 2015 Johannes Göransson
ISBN-13: 9781939460165
Printed and bound in the USA
Second Edition.

Tarpaulin Sky Press
P.O. Box 189
Grafton, Vermont 05146
www.tarpaulinsky.com

For more information on Tarpaulin Sky Press trade paperback and
hand-bound editions, as well as information regarding distribution,
personal orders, and catalogue requests, please visit our website at
tarpaulinsky.com.

Snart ska jag börja skriva hårdare, naknare, kortare.
Bortom dimman. Scener som överexponerade
fotografier. Dialoger som kunde vara fångade från en
övervakningskamera. Rörelser, fysik, behaviorism.
Jag längtar till det ljus som man kallar obarmhärtigt.
Jag är på väg dit.

—LARS NORÉN

# BURN THE WHOLE THING DOWN

Los Angeles tastes like iron in my mouth
and I blame my daughters,
for I'm feverish and they stand on the stairs and stare.
They have soiled mouths and blue eyes.
They are beautiful but disgusting because they break
the shells and carry sunflowers, thousands of sunflowers.
A daughter brings the inside outside
and the outside inside. A wife sits on the sofa
in the dark with mercury in her.
I love my wife because of the side effects.
I love my wife because the film has been poisoned
and she sealed it with a kiss and she brings me tiny
flowers with erect flower stalks and large seeds.
She might die in the movie. She might make it until
the enamel cracks. Might drive a car straight through
the feminine body.
Have you ever fallen in love while a city burned?
Then don't tell me that I'm sexist.
I'm writing a book
and I love the plastic chairs in which I sit.
I'm buying them with spit.

# THE MEADOW

We live in The Meadow but it's a hotel. We pay for it.
We call it The Meadow on account of the lamb masks.
And because of the sweet-smelling girl bodies on the sidewalk.
And because of my own tendency to affect the air
of a shepherd. Even during a time of plague-like symptoms,
I get murdered by the killer of little shepherds. Even during
a time of war that piles up bodies in sublime numbers,
I play the flute.

Die sunflowers die!

The faces are somewhat "disarticulated" due to "rat activity,"
according to the cops who study such things
to solve murders,
for example the murder of a Starlet
who shot videos of me at a shooting gallery.
That's me with the smeared fruit, doing that thing
with doll mouths.
We are making history.
We are using fucked up military time
while the riots expire. Look how many bodies we can pile up.
It's the national debt.

# THE STARLET IS DEAD

The Starlet is dead, we've seen her in a pool
and we've seen her in gun shows
they were playing shitty 80s music and crying
because once upon a time she had been
their beautiful Starlet. But not for years.
For years she had been shooting films that look
more like the lustgardens of suffering
or anatomies viewed through "private eyes."
They look like torture, said a cop who interrogated
me about my role in all of this.
My role was her secret star.
I was Duchess of Malfi
my body was smeared with apricots.
Nobody forced me to be there.
I was at a party that cops are re-creating with
new and less infected toys.
I praised them for the realism before I left.
They praised me for my foreskin.
I should have told them: Picture yourself
covered with cake, imagine how much it hurts.
They will never find her killer.
I hate cake.
Pretend I slit my wrists with nightingales.
I did it while listening to the Law. I did it to my wife while
all else failed. I had a tantrum but nobody died. I lied to
the camera in the Starlet's masterpiece, The Crime Flower.
I described a pair of beautiful panties

and pigeons skulls.
The panties belonged to a beautiful homeless
person I fucked with my left hand,
the pigeons belonged to capitalism.

# I DON'T HAVE TIME

Poetry is a waste because whores are already symbolic.
Whore bodies can scream or sing, and sometimes I imagine
their bodies smeared with rotten apricots. Like the ones
that covered my body at that horrible shooting range.
When you search for a killer, it is best not to scream. It's
best to have a working theory about bodies in Los Angeles.
My theory is not sound because it's all about book burnings
and screwy dolls.
I came up with it at a party for cops.
My daughters were hungry so I went and asked for some
mercury.

Girls are always mute but images
speak a thousand words – words like icky and ouch and
pretty and I wanted to cut her face up and so I cut a large
piece of gold paper.
An image might turn into a beautiful crane.
The image might contain radiation from the bomb.
Images might get people killed and I am in revenge movies.
In the sexual movie from a shooting range, the swans are
disgusting.

## KILLTEXT FOR UNDERAGE FANS

The thing about the hero is the hero is dead.
The thing is that lineages are supposed to move forward.
They are supposed to have a future.
Everybody knows that,
even the drowned immigrants lined up in the harbor.
The thing about them is that they just didn't make it
to the future.
The thing about me is that I talk like I have something
shoved in my mouth, which suggests that I belong there in
the harbor with the ship-wrecked. I don't have a future but I
have moths after sex.

I have a movie about Catholics.
It's a home movie and we're building something in the dirt.
The hero is dead of course. They call me Mr. Mass Grave on
the news and then they laugh kind of like how Asians
laugh in Asian movies about war. Hey that's not funny, says
the activist who actually has a kissing – yes KISSING! –
sickness. I've written a song about people like him,

but who cares. The hero is still dead and that makes my
daughters into something like, you know, non-daughters.
There can't be daughters if the hero is dead, can there? Can
there be Asian girls? My daughters are 3 and 6 and then there
are the other daughters, the ones who just seem to multiply
all the time while I'm out there searching for my killer. They
have lice in them and pretend to be virgins to the cops.

I'm searching the streets of Los Angeles.
Where my virginity is redundant.
Where we are stunted like the meadow which is full of lice
and mercury used to be a byproduct of progress.
That's why I only write with my mercury pen.
With my drippy pen. With my daughter pen. With snake
venom. With my raw meat. With my nature imagery. With
my blatant fuck-eye on you.

Can someone just get rid of poetry?

My daughters keep nagging me about the dripping in the wall.

Drip-drip-drip-drip-drip

It's my son.

The Riding Boy.

The White Death

I have been keeping my proverbial son in the rinse room out of a devotion to Art, by which I might mean something toxic. I have been keeping him out of it but I have also kept him locked up in it. He can't speak but he asks me questions with his body. He's made up his own spasmodic language with his body. He asks, Who's the girl with the branches? He asks, Who's the girl with the horse. He asks, Who's the girl with the hare? Why doesn't she have eyes? How does she move her mouth? What is the noise that comes out? Why is she so afraid? Why is she shaking? I begin to fear he's not actually talking about his sister but about something I once did in a hotel room, so I run away from my son, leaving him bruised there in his museum. When I leave, the rain leaves with me.

## THE LAW AGAINST FOREIGNERS INVOLVES MOSTLY THE BODY

I should know. I'm a foreigner and I want to live in Los
Angeles but Los Angeles just wants to take photographs
of my body when it's dank.
That's the weird part.
It's also interested in my body when dogs bark at my
genitals but it pretends that's just evidence of a social
conscience. It wants to find the human in me, even if it
takes ripping this lamb mask into a thousand shreds and
hanging it up on the wall.
And feign outrage when I go numb.
I leave good "teeth marks" I've been told.
I take a bad photograph because the model was hurt.
Poetry is like a bad photograph because the camera
doesn't work. Or a child is caught stealing from the
candy store. Caught fucking a homeless person.
I have a social conscience too and it makes me want to
burn the sheets after sex. It makes me scared of lice.
Poetry is so beautiful when it involves gasoline. Or when
it gives you a gun that clicks. A dead woman is the most
poetical topic in the world.

## HEART OF DARKNESS WOW

Shells are an omen in Los Angeles.
Fog is an omen in Los Angeles. Omen is a horror movie in
Los Angeles and Man is no exception. Shrunken skulls are
evidence of brutal romanticism; rock stars die.
The whole "noggin thing" is precious in Los Angeles.
Salt is also precious in Los Angeles but Passports are omens.
They are the worst. I hate my passport.
It doesn't even have my name in it. I look ugly like a criminal.
Ugly like a beautiful criminal and goosed up.
Every face is ugly in passports, it's part of the law.
My face is vile in Los Angeles, it's part of sexuality.
My body is precious in Los Angeles so CAKE IT UP.
In Los Angeles, a previous body is tasteless, we have to wash
the cake off, we have to give it feelings, a sense of interiority.
Art ruins everything yeah.
Poetry is supposed to give us inner lives but thank god,
things get ugly in Los Angeles
in large part because people die on mirrors here.
They vomit on their own image as a final act.
To America I only died yesterday.
The Starlet is not a Plaything.
The company doesn't lie it bones it dreams it covers up
the bodies in tarpaulin. Somewhere between hallucination
and Mexico, I have become a show-child.
During my show trial in Los Angeles, I was far more tender,
meat-wise. Drones have no stings.

While sitting around in my friend Martin's apartment,
I look over at his desk and happen to catch a glimpse
of the cover of a book about Francesca Woodman: a
photograph of three naked women with masks. One of
them is more full-bodied than the others and she also
wears mary-janes; she looks so sexy only the fact that I
am at a friend's house prevents me from jerking off on the
book. Instead I open it and start looking. I've seen some of
the photographs before but nonetheless they are gorgeous:
At times she appears as a rabid girl-child crawling around
an abandoned house, other times as a surrealist-ghost
figure on the verge of being absorbed by the walls, other
times as a pensive young woman, other times she is just
hot. Never does it seem like the figure is acting out of
an interior will. She seems caught up in the atmosphere
of the house. Perhaps it is wrong to focus on the young
woman entirely: she is made to be part of a material space,
the decaying atmosphere, which also includes the house,
flour-strewn floors, mirrors, dresses. This is why she
moves so strangely around the place: she is also part of
it. Is this one house or many houses? They are all part of
the same house. Just as the three beautiful women on the
cover are part of the ruined house. The ruin carries with
it an openness: it becomes more permeable than a modern
house. In other words, the ruin is more vulnerable to the
infestation of bodies. It cannot keep them out. Cannot
keep the girl out and cannot keep the camera out.

# I'M WORKING

Everything is arranged for the cameras.
The crameras. The shitty cram bodies burn like sheets.
Take the faces and thaw them or cover them up before
I go numb. Go "disarticulated" with crowns in front of
the camera.

White death moves across borders but I keep my son
locked up in an attic. I don't want him to be ruined
by disgusting Los Angeles so he's not allowed to speak;
he has to use gestures to explain his feelings. Don't take
that city and its awful language in your horrible mouth,
I tell him. But I think it's too late. Somehow a leading
man dies every time he makes the shuddery sign for get
me out of here. It's the dirty bird hello.

My wife on the other hand is writing a treatise on
photography parties from the 1980s, but she has white
stuff smeared on her fingers. I'm thinking, I hate
evidence but I love clues.

There is a law against photographing a father.
My daughters are doing it again and the horse
has many holes in it.
Something so shitty should be disco
Discos burn down with immigrants inside
Poetry burns down with me inside

The music is the same: Los Angeles, dirty bird, I'll be your deer-heart on the asphalt.
I'll be your mirror. I'll be your allegory about immigration. I'll be your body about death. Fox deaths and latex deaths.

## POEM WRITTEN ON A MIRROR

The aesthetic of Los Angeles seems based on whore-nature
and victory dances.
And everything looks stuffed into bags
or makes you feel like you're stuffed in a plastic bag and dead.
Even when I'm having my hair done in Los Angeles,
I think about carrying mammals in plastic bags.
I think about the latest riot and black bodies look so hot
on TV. There is so much fluid in them wow.

I think about barbwire and 24 hours of children.
48 hours of children. 72 hours of children.
A whole lifetime measured out in graphic bodies.

Maybe I can muffle Los Angeles a little better. I can write
about Capitalism and Art. And maybe I can describe
why I hate what you have done with my cocaine.
Poetry is a drug: I've heard that before.
Poetry is a drag: the body gets all chapped in the hot sand
and the natives are furious and violent and the schlong
hangs out.
You can take a photograph of me and post it on the
Internet: here is Johannes
passed out on a mirror. In Somalia.

This morning a beautiful fog covered the streets of the city. Everyone was either a jogger or homeless. One jogger's ass reminded me of a girl I knew in grad school. One homeless woman wore the kind of skirt made for finger-fucking in a cab. At first I thought my soul was as pure as an advertising girl with glossy lips, but then I thought something ugly was going on. If I was a girl, I think I'd be the kind of girl I wouldn't want to fuck with my fingers. I've broken some kind of mirror. With my fingernails I'm clawing at the partition. I'm looking for a window to look at. To admire. To break. Poetry is just a man speaking to men. Skin is just a woman.

My son is a foreign body, which makes him beautiful
in Los Angeles where my wife and I live with sperm on
our hands and bellies.
My daughters are disgusting with Los Angeles.
It's in their hair and on their lips.
We want to keep my son safe from Los Angeles
so we shut him up.
We let him play with a rocking chair and his body
but not with language which feels like petals
in your beautiful mouth
when you interrogate prisoners.
They may look like corpses in photographs
but in Los Angeles they look allegorical.
All day. All allegory. Now you enter the city of fully
1,500,000, the largest in "The Flowery Kingdom." You
are really on Chinese soil and amid Chinese institutions.
How quaint and curious everything is! A Chinese city
is the most bewildering place in the world. The streets
of Canton are mere alleys, not over six or eight feet
wide, on an average, yet lined with bazars, through
which entrance is had to the dwellings above. There
are no carts, drays and cars. Porters do the dray work
on their shoulders or in barrows and push-carts. The
passenger vehicle is the Sedan-chair, made lightly of
bamboo and covered with awning. The Chinese have
great reverence for parents. They worship fathers and
grandfathers. This sentiment is shown in the names of
their streets. There are streets in Canton of such names

as "One Hundred Grandsons," "Thousand Beatitudes," "Everlasting Love," "Thousand Peace," "Ninefold Brightness," "Market of Golden Profits," "Saluting Dragons" and so on.

# IDOLS IN THE TEMPLE OF THE JUGGERNAUT

I steal some curtains from the theater to illustrate
The Law of the True Meaning.
I love that law.
It's so beautiful it can slaughter half of Baghdad.
It's so beautiful it fucks homeless people.
Unfortunately, that does not include the dead woman,
even if she has big tits.
It also does not include a billboard of my anorexic mask
going to shit like insects. These figures belong to some
other law, one that is less hopeful.
Look out so you don't get aids from fucking the mask!
Look out so that the girls don't go all hoochie coochie
with petals in their mouths!
It's more like the law of treason or the law of dead
children than the law of true meaning.
I like all of them because I love laws and I love to fuck
women. I want to cover every naked woman with black
cocaine in my blood. I want to fuck Eva Braun.
These are the wrong laws, Violent Flower!
These are laws from the Crime Bed!
I can't sleep in this crime bed. I want to receive flowers
and blowjobs. My dick is too hard and my eyes too blind
from medicine.
Everything is turning beautifully white.
My wife has petals in her mouth and in her ass and she is
reading about Maldoror.

After sex we'll wrap our clammy white bodies in the curtain. There's a picture I've drawn on the curtain, it's kind of ugly – like rat flower – because I was high when I drew it.
How embarrassing to be a rat-catcher in a flowery kingdom. How embarrassing to act like I am a lawyer when I simply write torture memos.
Beautiful little memos about the orient.

## THE CUT:

For you I will write pigs in blood on the refrigerator door.
For you I will eat pork on my birthday.
For you I will eat pork on your grave.
For you I will puke up pork in the Green Zone.
For you I will grease up the naked ladies on film.
For you I will pork out images and images are like dead
pigs in the road.
For you I die when I go outside of Los Angeles. I'm
wrapped in a curtain and my face is ridiculous with
morning. There's no telling who's a foreigner in Los
Angeles, but the minute we leave we blind. Outside Los
Angeles we're ugly and we don't have any more pigs. And
we opened the bottomless pit.... And there came out of the
smoke locusts upon the earth; and unto them was given
power, as the scorpions of the earth have power... The
scorpion will prevail. Anger will prevail.... My wife drains
a glass of wine and a bit of it dribbles down her chin. It's
like summer will never end.

Every time I make an image of myself an angel masturbates.
Every time I try to escape from Los Angeles a killer learns
how to crawl. Sick.

## THE TRUE SUBJECT

In all likelihood, my true subject is Fame
and its war brides.
Isn't Fame really about meaning?
I want someone to write a poem that dissects me
like a rotten animal on a table.
But that's not going to happen, not now that the Starlet is
dead, so I'll have to make my own pornography.
I'm not an animal, I yell but my mouth is full.
My son tells me to stop.
He tells me with his fists and his tears and his screaming.
I am dead in Los Angeles and my son loves the funeral.
I am shivering cold because I feel too much.
For example, about my wife who has tits in Los Angeles.
She wraps me in the curtain.
The pussy, lets call it.

# THE LAW OF THE IMAGE

In The Law there's an image of me as nothing but myself.
I look obese. I am more than myself.
I'm lying there on a mirror reading The Law Against
Images of Myself.
I'm looking at myself.
I look criminal with all this media on my face,
the white powder all up in my nose and on my lips.
Los Angeles invented this media to destroy bodies.
Los Angeles invented bodies that it could not control
for they were driven by an occult force: Fame.
I invented my son to destroy Los Angeles.
When I run out of my son's room I bring the rain with me.
The image is a flower that opens up
in a drowning victim's mouth.
If there's such a thing as Poetry it should taste like that
flower. It should feel like water on one's naked skin.
But it feels like a curtain instead.
Sweaty and someone has drawn lewd images on the velvet.
Someone has cut a strip out to stuff in my mouth. It tastes
like Victory. Poetry has to destroy Los Angeles.
Poetry has to be Los Angeles. Fat City. The wheels
never stop spinning, the blood never stops circulating.
It's like summer will never end. In the dark we hear the
grasshoppers scratching their legs. Our daughters are all
sleeping on a "Chinese bed."

Like the damaged tool, I can't be of use anymore. I've become an image of myself. Or an image of a tool, a hammer that is supposed to be used to destroy icons. But it's cracked. Of course it's also not at all "like a tool" because I'm not a "tool" at all. I'm a cadaver.

## THE ROTTEN HEART OF SIN IS EXQUISITELY MANNERED

Homeless people are good for images, photographers love
them. I find them disgusting when they get killed and when
they fuck they smell really bad on your dick.
Swans on the other hand are beautiful when they burn in
crime movies.
In this crime movie, we're at the shooting range again.
Imagine all that apricot mess, all those ridiculous
ornaments. All that pork. We can't leave. We don't have
the proper documentation.
Images get in the way of dignity, poets tell me. Poetry
gets in the way of money, whores tell me. I fuck both and
I don't even have to pay. I've got that card: Get out of jail
free. Exterminate the brutes yeah.

KILL ALL THE POETS BECAUSE THEY
ARE RICH

## BERLIN

Some say I'm an idiot.
Some say I'm an idiot because I go nightclubbing like a new
person who is dead and young and totally covered in chalk.
I go: I have a virgin body!
I go to the innocence riots with nose-blood.
I'm an idiot because I care. I'm a sexist because I love tits
and I'm on television. Look: I'm white-clubbing!
I am opening up an old wound with
my gladiolus. I'm pretending that I know the way out of here.
Poetry only leads us further into cattle. Poetry gives us
poisonous flowers, which we feed to the cattle. Poetry is
swines that we feed pearls. How can we afford to write poetry
while the corpses pile up in the streets?
Poetry is playing with corpses.
This is the spit scene.

## THE SPIT SCENE

We still can't figure out what to do with the body.
My wife wants to bring the plague inside the auditorium.
Sara wants to remake Francesca Woodman with cocaine.
I will photograph both of them with my shitty
phone-camera. I know what you are thinking,
you are thinking: What will you do with the camera that
hasn't already been done with a fist, Crime Flower?
I know you think it's no longer feasible to make corpses in
the street, but I have no other choice.
They are posing for me.
Don't tell me it's pornography or tell me it's pornography,
everything is porn if you look hard enough.
Every corpse in the street is an image of itself.
I'm shooting every one of them with my rifle.
And the riot isn't even over!

# FANTASIES ABOUT THE RUINS OF LOS ANGELES

## THE FLOWERY KINGDOM

It is almost impossible to describe the imperial palace with
its nine great courts, marble doors and roofs glittering
in gold. Its largest court is for the Emperor alone. It
is surrounded by an immense gallery, in which are the
treasure magazines. One contains models of all the metal
work in the kingdom; a second contains specimens of
the finest furs; the third, robes of every variety; a fourth,
pearls, rare marbles and precious stones; a fifth the
wearing apparel of the Emperor and royal family; the rest
are depots for arms taken in battle and royal presents.

VARIOUS POSES IN THE LAW:

I was terrified.
I was silver.
I was a virgin.
I was war.
I was marble.
I was people.
I was opium.
I was over.
I was famous.
I was dogs.
I was hooded.
I was towers.
I was genital.
I was symbolic.
I was Chinese.
I was souvenirs.
I was nostalgic.
I was mystical.
I was medical.
I was glorified.
I was mutilated.
I was mythical.
I was copies.
I was submarine.
I was hermaphrodites.
I was smiling.

I was away.
I was fossils.
I was visual.
I was extinct.
I was fun.

My wife is bathing my head with a rag soaked in vodka and smearing my cum on my chest to help numb out the throbbing. She wipes up the nosebleed with her silk glove. One day I will go where people live. I have already seen: the hospitals. One day I will see: where people come to die. One day, I will totally invent a language with which I will teach the defeated how to speak like an idiot with golden eyelashes. I will taunt the crowd. I will ruin everything with my stupid "hellos." For now I'm going to put on my jeans. I'm going to look partied in my ugly face. Winter is coming. Everywhere in our apartment my daughters have left their crass reminders: underwear, crayons, plastic bags of muck, and drawings of dead girls and pandas. I'm the Father.

PARTY

We only have two options in art so why fight all the time?
Because we only have one option.
Personally I want to make porn from Japan or the Winter
Palace. *After* I've been busted as Capitalism's court jester
(and not a very good one at that, always stoned like a
fuck-up and listening to rap from the 90s).
Where's the great dead white man when you need someone
to feed the crowd with the cake?
Meanwhile, I'm thinking about revenge porn.
Here we are now entertain us with asbestos.
That's my libido speaking.
Sometimes I really am a teenager.
That's my anorexia speaking.

# I WANT TO KEEP THE CAMERA OUT

when I attempt to complicate my landscape fetish
but then I start to think about tits
and the law against paying your taxes
because I love the illustrations of the riots.
The Law is pretty clear when it comes to collapsing in public.
The mobs are pretty because all my money is in foreign
currencies – i.e. rat music – and I tend to faint.
I tend to have these black ribbons... funeral possessions...
I tend to hate men's bodies. It's what makes me the ideal
reader of the law.
I read it with convictions and I have a hard-on.
You can carry me through the riots with my hard on.
You can call me Crime Flower this autumn.
You can look infected in your mouth if you let me look
infected in my money.
I need teenagers to look even more repulsive
like presidents.
I need them to eat candy in memory of my dead friend.
... It's like a welcome-back party for a soldier who'd been
eating pork at the whore-palace of Baghdad.
Women's spit looks best at sunset, men's bodies look best
when pale stuff is coming in through the cracked window in
my study. Where I keep my skulls and roses to demonstrate
that I don't belong.
I belong.
I belong.
Los Angeles has many dummies.

## TORCH SONG

I think athletes are the new road kill.
Anybody wearing a Reagan mask can fuck me
but not because I love Reagan.
I love operas and maybe serial killers.
I wish I had a porcelain body
but I have something more bruised.
I wish I owned a butcher shop.
Once I had a concussion and another time a photo shoot
went all wrong and we had to cover things up before we left
the hotel room.
Last night I dreamt that my angry friend Matt put his little
dick inside a syringe in order to prove a point.
I think I'm the real culprit but not in a direct sense.
Imagine an underground chamber...
necks fastened... puppet shows...
I want to throw our stuffed squirrel in the fire
but my daughters won't let me. They're in love with America.
They have a winter fever. I have a wound in the snow.
I wish I could sell some silkscreens.
Fever silks, I could call them.
My wife wants to drape me in silk. She wants to use braille
and I'm paranoid about fucking homeless people.
And I'm paranoid about virgins: nobody ever
watches that film. I've watched the film
and now I feel half-born, like I could lacerate.
My secret cobra.
My swollen clitoris.

## PROTEST ART

At a protest, I heard a loud bang and there was smoke coming from a girl next to me and then she fell to the ground and she was bleeding out of her torso. One man filmed her body, her face. She whispered "help me mamma" as blood trickled out of her pretty mouth. And then she died. Later that night, the images spread across the Internet, stoking further protests, prompting the governor to make a televised appearance, in which he denounced the footage as art.

I spent the day watching TV with the kids. In one show an adult man who lived in a land of puppets received a box. He couldn't figure out what the box did, so he asked the puppets. One puppet suggested it was some kind of doorstop but the adult man did not think so, the box was too pretty for such a utilitarian purpose. One puppet suggested that there might be a whelk inside the box, that they needed to free the whelk. But there is probably not enough air in the box, said the man. I was starting to feel increasingly angsty about the box when suddenly the TV channel broke to news of a mall where a group had started to shoot people. Were still shooting people. We could hear the shooting on the TV from outside the mall. What was going on inside the mall? Bodies piled up. Black bodies. The event took place someplace else but maybe not. My daughters started freaking out. They wanted to find out what was in the box. They seemed to blame me for ruining their show. As if I had fired the rifles. I told them there was a toy inside the box. What kind of toy? A toy for fighting.

MORE PHOTOS:

Naked man with dogs
heap of naked men with dogs
man with Disney
man with mask on genitals
woman
with rubber gloves
man with bag over head
woman with bright lips
frightening chair
bra over face
armless woman
"Surrounded by Snakes"
Electric Chair
Decoy on the Street
"After a riot..."
Porcelain looks cracked
Woman glistens in her pussy
Hairy woman
Woman who hates mirrors
Woman who loves men with bags over their heads
Woman shot in dark with a murky quality
The Ghost of a Flea
Saturn Devouring His Son
Butterfly horrors
Animal Crossings
The Parrot's Perch
"Christ's Crown"

Now my wife appears to have passed out on the bed.
She seems to have placed a glowing spider
web over her thighs.
The smell of kerosene from the outside
merges with the smell of my wife's sweaty body.
She has strangely thin ankles. She's thinking about war.
She must be. She is speaking in her sleep about marrows
in snow. She's mumbling about vermin. She says
something about me wearing dress shoes that get wet in
the snow. "Bay of Pigs." Red twilight.

Let's be literal about our translations.
Let's be faithful to the rotting python.

## BUG TIME (FOR AYLIN)

Children smell bad and there is no justice. RIP.

EXTERMINATE THE BRUTES!

There are gangs in the rape fields of Los Angeles
because there are sons.
Killers are beautiful in Los Angeles because they care.
That and because they are white.
Beautiful like a killer in the sun, as that one song says.
It's a date song, I've heard.
Face the rat music!
Up against the wall rat face!
Faces are important because they have mouths and eyes
and sometimes they are chewing on disgusting meats in
my house.
I have one daughter I call our "outside daughter."
But most of them are "inside daughters."
Too bad they are constantly coming and going and
getting sick all over our floor. I should make them all
outside daughters. They make me sick.
My wife is definitely an inside wife. She sits in the couch
and is almost dead from mercury poisoning, aka Art.
... bloated cadaver of the bourgeoisie... I am the one in
the greaser room... nazi glamour... Dear friend, I see
your pig lips and your pig eyes and your pretty pink
body everywhere I go. Dear Los Angeles, stop cutting
yourself, I'm not you.

I wish my son would just go to sleep. He's constantly clanking that horse against the wall or the door, moaning. When I come in he draws more images in the air: knife, flower, secret code, dance that makes his head tilt and hit the wall. He's trying to tell me that there's murdering going on in the streets, that rioters are tearing down statues of the governor, that they're following a secret code, like a disease. He's not telling me anything I don't know. He can't. Everything he knows he gets from me. That's why I keep him locked up.

Reproduction:
Flowering Locus C
Carrion Flowers
Stinking Flowers
Corpse Flowers
The Odor of Decaying Meat
Hyena Flowers
Dogs of War
Calliflorid Flies
Flesh flies
Inflorescence
Night Visitors
Female Bees

AT THE SHRINE FOR THE DEAD STARLET:

Card #1:
Dear Starlet,

You meant so very much to me. I remember watching your first movie with my parents when they were still together. You were so pretty with your nearly latin features – dark eyes, dark hair. I just watched that movie again and I imagined that you were still alive, were still that young, and my parents were still together, and I was still a little girl who hadn't done all these awful things that I have done. It seems the past has caught up with us both.

Card #2:
Dear Breathless Lovely Starlet,

We will do everything to catch your killer. We will demand justice. We will demand to see your body. We will protest until we find out the truth about your body.

Card #3:
Dear Detective,

I know who killed the Starlet. Find me at the Heart of Glamour.

I don't know what "the heart of glamour" is, so I make
a map of Los Angeles based on a glamorous body. I
superimpose the body on a map I bought in a tourist
shop – a kind of oversized dollhouse that was hit hard by
the riots. They were selling water-damaged rooster-heads
whose gilding-paper had been charred, at half price;
and they were selling butterflies with holes in them for
even less. *Wosh-wosh* went the banged-up loudspeakers.
"It's the *blood tsunami*," whispered the woman behind the
counter and winked at me.

# THE HEART OF GLAMOUR

In the heart of glamour is a slaughterhouse;
they are killing pigs on a conveyor belt. It's impossible
to translate. Translation is impossible but
it happens all the time in capitalism.
Here's an attempt: Capitalism produces meat.
In the meat productions we act the part of
whores of Baghdad and we act like teenagers in
a swimming pool. We are sexy
but the shattered glass cuts and the pigs smell
of chlorine. We kill pigs but we can't kill Capitalism.
We can kill pigs and we can kill my arms or
legs or china or tracheas but we can't
kill capitalism. We can kill poetry. It smells like black
milk. It smells like whores. We can kill poetry.
We can kill poetry like teenagers. Fuck it over and over
while pigs are slaughtered. The whores are expensive
like cancer. Abu Ghraib is the capitol of the 21st century,
sex is its flower. In my poetry I fuck the whores
with a camera - I'm an extraordinary journalist – but
I need to find the marrow before I can write it all
down. The poetry. The poetry. The slaughter is a kind
of translation. Translation is impossible because the
marrow is impossible to find in all this pig. Translation is
impossible poetry in all this pig.

I am learning poetry in the heart of glamour.
I'm learning that the pigs were guilty
and that's why they had to be given injections
that disoriented them on the way to grinder.

I'm learning that the injections make them convulse
and they crack their heads against the floor.

And I'm learning that the map doesn't work or I don't
know how to translate Los Angeles. There are too many
bodies but I've never been to the opera and I'm not about
to leave.

The sublime comes from the failure of math!

I can't count all the bodies and I can't count with my
fingers because they are blurry and my orpheus face is
turning out all wrong. I feel like I'm drowning. Images of
drowning come in many colors but here, in the heart of
glamour, the clamorous cocoon of fuck-bodies, they are
swine-colored.

They are whore-paradise at night.

The teenagers are strewn with gossamer.
I'd rather stand here and try to translate the translation
of pigs.
I love rabbits, I think, because their eyes are less milky
except when they have rabies or children.

But all the pigs are guilty: they have raped girls and
buried them alive. As punishment they are injected in
their scrotums but their bodies continue to convulse and
they hit their faces against the cement so their jaws hang

from their heads but they can't do anything about it because they have been injected in their scrotums.

Isn't it gross to show images of scrotums?

Yes, it's obscene so the meat producers cover up the scrotums when they are injected and then they tell the journalists to get out when the journalists are trying to get a picture of the scrotum as it is injected with the milk that will make the pigs go all spastic but won't kill them just keep them somewhat out of it as they are slaughtered and ground into meat.

Their hair feels soft like as a teenager's pubic hair.

"Wosh-wosh," hums my daughter along with the machines.

I have a thousand-year tattoo to go with my puppy-soft orpheus mask.

I let the champagne bleed a little like the meat before I drink it.

A toast to the remix!

Before the pigs are killed they have to be cleansed with a cleansing fluid that smells like chlorine. When the pigs are injected with milk in their scrotums I demand that

a famous actress should play dead in the production but
the meat producers say nobody famous can play the pig
because they are criminal pigs they have gang-banged
a girl and buried her alive so they have to be played by
piggy pigs.

Wosh-wosh blood tsunami!

In the piggy heart of glamour the audience gasps because
my dick is so pretty.

I am asked what dish I like better.

It tastes like iron.

I can feel the butterflies swarming around my cuts.

If Sara was here to photograph me she would probably
name this moment Mother.

She would probably make it into surveillance porn:

> Silver fishes have abdomens that taper at the end,
> which makes them look like fishes even though they
> are insects. They inhabit moist areas. They are often
> found on rape victims.

Some rape victims are buried alive after they have been
gang-banged.

The male silverfish's semen is covered in gossamer.
The female lays groups of fewer than 60 eggs at once,
deposited in small crevices.

I don't know anything about insects!
I'm a singer with a beautiful voice!
I'm a croak-singer in the Heart of Glamour!

Be careful, the meat producer tells me and points to
my legs, the pigs can smell blood and it drives them
crazy! I don't know why my legs are bloody – probably
from kicking in the windows at a playground. What
about all this blood on the sluice-floor? I ask him. No
it is just human blood that drives them crazy. They can
smell it and they want to eat it like they are eating each
other's ears. So a beautiful whore wipes off my legs
with cleansing fluid like we were in a catholic mass or
a catholic convulsionary. Don't drive them crazy says a
whore.

I take it she wants a role in the production.
I take it she wants to play the part of an angel or a rabbit.
I take it she wants my orpheus mask for its tickly tongue.
I'm almost deaf from all these screaming doves.
I'm holding a box of bees that may be used to inject
poison into pigs scrotums
in representations of this event.
It smells like milk and honey.

Why are all these pigs in here, I ask, I thought this would
be more like a strip club. I'm joking because I'm getting
nervous about all these scrotums. Someone suggests
using tape on the scrotums and I suggest they get rid of
all the silver fish because silver fish eat books.

I can hear the trucks driving by!
I imagine they are crystal ships.

You know what I mean, you fucking killer of
berlin-shepherds!
You buried live girls.
You brought them back with intrusion music.
Your mouth tastes like strawberry from lipstick.
And cunt from cunts.
And flowers from saints.

Because I've been eating rice porridge
because it's white
and I'm poisoned in movies about Asia!

I have an eye infection and it's called Art when I turn
around I see you breathing with a tube because you can't
stand it in here. I can't stand the scrotums in here! I hate
the pig smell and the pig flowers look like scrotums and
I don't want to see those kinds of flowers, I want to see
pussy and fuck pussy. Everything gets in the way.

My daughter tugs on my arm

and wants to watch a show about
ponies and asks why the skin
itches it must itch on the pigs
because they are biting each other
in their thick skins and their ears
it must be because it itches
they are eating each other like
a fucking gang bang while
the camera snaps pictures of my face

My mouth is so beautiful when I spit
and my eyes are so pretty
when they see absolutely nothing
but thorn-roses and milk

I walked into the Heart of Glamour with a dazzling
thought in my head: I was going to find the killer who
killed the Starlet. But instead I am watching piles and
piles of pig get ground up for raping women. I see piles
of pigs getting their scrotums injected with milk and
honey. I'm lost in this heart of flowers. This anymore-
heart of shining meat which will be devoured around
swimming pools.

We'll sell it as the New Imagery.
New Baghdad.
We'll sell it for a low low price
because everyone is poor now everyone
is starving now (naive for sure, inspired by babies

perspired like hot-bodies, shouted like ship-wrecks, bright like mommy in the morning, faint like a father wrapped in veils, fish like a cutting board, seconds like hands, white like umbrellas, cut like my nostrils, old like Alzheimer's, passengers like exterminate the bores, worshipped like teenagers, finished like dictators, fat like mice, buried like sand on a rape victim, skinny like my left eye, owner like orders, snuggly like a sun's hard things, crying like black, scrotum like disheveled, stare like pig).

I look at my orpheus mask like it's prison sex.

I look at my orpheus mask like it's knocked out.

I lack all context and that's why I'm porny in the surveillance footage.

Who brought the revolvers? Who smoked the last bowl? Who is going to be shot in the head? Who is going to make a narrative out of these clues?

Click on the picture of a bait.

I have a dream.

This is a kind of paradise.

I'm going out to fetch the little calf.

You come too.

# THE HEART OF GLAMOUR

I just wanted to say thanks to all who have supported me over the years: Reverend Campbell, for my spiritual guidance; Aaron, the father of Darrian, my son; and Maurie, my attorney. Thank you everybody. This is not a loss, this is a win. You know where I am going. I am going home to be with Jesus. Keep the faith. I love y'all. Thank you, Chaplain.

I just want to say I don't want you to have hate in your heart for me, because I took your loved one. I know it doesn't mean anything; I told the truth because I feel like you should know who killed your loved one. God watches everything. Don't hate me, if you do, you'll have to deal with Him later. For me, live your life but don't hate me. I'm sorry for taking your loved one.

Ms. Suzy, Susan, thank you for fighting for me in the courts. Thank you for supporting me for all these years. Elroy Chester wasn't a bad man, I knew me. A lot of people say I didn't commit those murders, I really did it. That's my statement. Warden, you can go ahead.

You clown police. You gonna stop with all that killing all these kids. You're gonna stop killing innocent kids, murdering young kids. When I kill one or pop one, y'all want to kill me. God has a plan for everything. You hear? I love everyone that loves me. I ain't got no love for anyone that don't love me.

First of all; Shonna talk to your brother. He'll tell you the truth about what happened to your husband. I told Bubba to tell you what happened. Now, my statement to the world: I am in the midst of truth. I am good, I am straight, don't trip. To all my partners, tell them I said like Arnold Schwarzenegger, "I'll be back." These eyes will close, but they will be opened again, my understanding of God is, Jesus has got me through. To my family, I love y'all.

Life is death, death is life. I hope that someday this absurdity that humanity has come to will come to and an end. Life is too short. I hope that anyone that has negative energy towards me will resolve that. Life is too short to harbor feelings of hatred and anger. That's it.

To my loved ones and dear friends, I love y'all and appreciate y'all for being there. I am going to a better place. To all the guys back on the row, keep your heads up, keep up the fight. I am ready. Let's go.

Ms. Connie Hilton, I'm sorry for what happened to you. If I hadn't raped you, then you wouldn't have lived. If you look at the transcripts, I didn't kill Mr. Newman and I didn't rob your house. There are two people still alive. I was just there. When I saw you in the truck driving away, I could have killed you but I didn't. I'm not a killer. My momma was abused. I'm sorry for what you've gone through. It wasn't me that harmed and stole all of your stuff. If you look at the transcripts you will see. I ask the good Lord to forgive me.

I love y'all; Sheena, my sister, momma, and daddy. Y'all pray for me, keep up the fight. Get the transcripts, let the truth come out so that I do not die in vain. I thank the Lord for the man I am today. I have done all I can to better myself, to learn to read and write. Take me to my King. I love y'all and thank you for the love you gave me. I respect all of y'all. Ms. Hilton. Ok. Let me rest. It's burning.

Hey mom and pop. I love y'all, all of you people in there. You know, y'all have to come together, you too Terrella. Y'all work on that. We all have to stand before God at the end of the day. Don't ever think you're perfect, none of us are perfect. God is the only one that is perfect. Jesus is perfect. I did wrong, now I am paying the ultimate price, even though it's a crooked way. I don't hate y'all. Don't judge, I'm not judging. God has to judge those people. I forgive. Always remember, Romans 12:19 is for real, hell is for real. If y'all don't have your life right, get it right. We all have to die to get to heaven. Get your life right with Christ; it's coming to an end. I'm talking to each and every soul in this building, in this room. I don't hate nobody, you're doing what you think is your job. God's law is above this law.

Hang on. Cowboy up, I'm fixing to ride. Jesus is my ride. Tell my babies, daddy will look down on them. Put a "C" in his name for Carl. Tell my boys and tell Tracy to keep on keeping on. Love one another, go to church, change your life for Christ, live your life for Christ. All right, Warden. Terella, I feel it babe, love.

Can you hear me? Did I ever tell you, you have dad's eyes? I've noticed that in the last couple of days. I'm sorry for putting you through all this. Tell everyone I love them. It was good seeing the kids. I love them all; tell mom, everybody. I am very sorry for all of the pain. Tell Brenda I love her. To everybody back on the row, I know you're going through a lot over there. Keep fighting, don't give up everybody.

*Afterwards:*

My daughter tells me that the proximity of electroshock treatment can cause sterility. That is why psychiatrists so seldom have children; or if they do, why the children are so often black children that have been adopted from Africa. This must also be why the employees at the slaughterhouse wear masks on their genitals and why they still have trouble conceiving – whether male or female – and why, if they do manage to give birth, the children are small and covered with a light fuss. I tell my daughter: "You think you know so much. Why don't you help your mother and me find the Killer!" And she says: "I'll creep into it and from there I'll tell you where to find the killer. If you buy me a caddy-lack"

Woke up early and went to the store to buy some breakfast, but it was too early so I walked around the neighborhood. Saw posters for "Too Cute to Puke" and "Young, Lean, Sad Boys" and for the showing of the movie *The Act of Killing*, in which the director, Josh Oppenheimer, convinces mass murderers in Sumatra to re-stage their murders of labor organizers as musicals. I would love to see it, though I feel like I already have such a beautiful idea of it in my mind that maybe I would ruin it by seeing the real thing. Then I got a cup of latte in the café and then the store was open but I just could not think of what to get, so I just got a bottle of yogurt. Everything else was beneath me.

## THE PIG PROTEST

So we make a new map based on a car crash
and we walk to the victim's eyes
and there we find a women's health clinic.
Protesters are wielding little fetus toys. They're in love
with death. You can tell by the way they burn soft bodies.
And the way they burn an effigy of the president.
I watch them on the surveillance camera – the camera
makes them look beautiful. I'm in love with gasoline
but I can't drink it. Not yet. I can't douse my daughter either
even though this city wants to kill her. I can't look.
My daughters will suck black milk out
of this city's whore-nature and maybe they will survive
while I read game-poems about genocide.
"No one really dreams any longer of the blue flower,"
begins a description of a children's game in which one
person is the flower and one is the hammer; the rest are
mouths. The one with the most cuts wins. The one who falls
asleep wins. The one who is covered in garbage bags has
to sweep up. The one who puts the bodies back together
is called poet or prisoner. I want to pick every body apart
again but I also want to exterminate every fucking thing,
leave nothing behind. That's what art tells me to do. The
poet or prisoners love art and will do anything it tells them
to. They love me, they love me, they love me.

It is easy to be true to Los Angeles: All mammals are
susceptible to Disease.
The public body must be punished because it has holes in it.
The teenagers are high: dunk, dunk.
They wear the same beautiful jewelry I wear.
Kill your darlings, says Sara and I notice that I'm bleeding
from my wrist.
I want movies to be blind, I tell her.
Sugar blind, I tell her.
Cum blind, she tells me while wiping some snot from her face.
Exterminate this shit, she tells me like she was an angel.
The helicopters make me think about the movies,
buying shit makes me think about the riots.
Can you hear me, asks Sara.
There is a road in Los Angeles called Silk Road
where the cuts are teeming... The bomb fits...

One daughter's eyes are black with flies. I have to shoo the flies away just to get food into her mouth.

Our daughter, Arson, is singing a song about becoming a landscape painted and littered with bodies. It's a song about growing up, becoming her father's daughter.

It's a message for inmates. I fear she's pregnant.

# BEAUTIFUL SUICIDE MUSIC

My wife says about the third Big Star record: "beautiful suicide music."

Dreams and wishes are like white.

I want to sleep all day today... nothing can hurt me...

I want the Sepulchral Chambers of The Law to be decorated with cunts, roaches.

I can't feel anything even though... well, the "reverse wound" isn't such a catchy phrase... And it's nightmare night in Ponyville.

I want a new pair of sneakers: white and soft.

I'm not trying to sell the 21$^{st}$ century because I'm too sleepy and I believe in Jesus Christ... Blame the game, not the gouge bodies.

Everybody smiles about civil rights but nobody wants to shake my hand.

My catacomb hand.

It's the hand I use during tantrums and to make screwy dolls.

At first I feared that I would be next but now I think the killer doesn't even know who I am. I am a "pillow angel."

Here I come. Better watch your step.

I'm going to break your heart in two.

# HADES PARTY

The violence of Fame makes itself known in bodies.
Fame looks allegorical but then what doesn't anymore?
The contents look damaged in media.
This one hot bitch has been cut
like horses whose mouths are bleeding.
The wig is on the pavement and it's discolored.
Tonight we look at pictures of rotten fruit.
Tonight someone wanted to hurt me.
Spumey fuck, they said and they meant it.
They had seen me reclining in a Chinese bed.
Sara, they had seen me
in the station light. I was surrounded
by ten thousand cars.
We had tasers supposedly.
I call them electric swans and sell them to prostitutes.
I have a long interview with one such whore.
We talk about the cold war
and my hallucinations are ridiculous
and then we talk about the girl corpses in
the street and then we talk about ambrosia
and the rumors about girl corpses and restaurants...
He tells me that poetry is better in the silent era.
You have to be beaten to death by cops, he tells me.
I tell him I don't understand.
He tells me he wants to be a CEO.
Of what, I ask him. Winter, he says. Ugh, I say.
Fuck you, he says. Winter is the new winter.

My daughters keep bringing butterflies into our room. I don't mind the fluttering against my face but I don't like the stench from rotten oranges and how insects seem to swarm around the oranges as if they were open wounds. In the middle of sex, more and more butterflies land on my wife's naked spine. Once we had sex in a fox-hole abandoned by soldiers. Once we fucked in red riot-lights.

Noctuid moths have drab forewings, although some have brightly colored hind wings. The overwhelming majority of noctuids fly at night and are almost invariably strongly attracted to light. Many are also attracted to sugar and nectar-rich flowers. Some of the family are preyed upon by bats. However, many Noctuidae species have tiny organs in their ears that responds to bat echolocation calls, sending their wing muscles into spasm and causing the moths to dart erratically. This aids the moths in evading the bats. Several species have larvae (caterpillars) that live in the soil and are agricultural or horticultural pests. These are the "cutworms" that eat the bases of young brassicas and lettuces. They form hard, shiny pupae. Most noctuid larvae feed at night, resting in the soil or in a crevice in its food plant during the day.

One daughter looked horrified when she witnessed me and her mother trying to prod out a videotape that had gotten stuck in the machine. When we got it out, the black tape-matter was all unspooled and crinkled up. We tried to wind it up but it was wrecked. Then we looked up and saw our daughter who had a horrified expression on her face. It was a primal scene. The next day we found her trying to repeat the experience on her brother.

## NOTES

This song must have been recorded during a plague like our own. I can tell from the imagery: blowtorch, cocoon, theater. It must have been a hit because it moves me. I want to dance.

❋

I'm teaching my daughters about prisoners, but they just want to play hide-and-seek. It's 1983. Pure biography.

❋

I want to bring cold war back to art: its pale, tortured white body, its teenagers, its Japanese prostitutes, its gash and glory, its parties. Its parties. Everything is an interview. Yideum asks me why I'm cold.

❋

How I Lived and What I Lived For:
Puking silk
A sniper kept a nightingale under his bed
My fave sitcom
Surrender monkeys
Seduced by Fame and Hospitals
Sedition

*

It's hard to hear what people are saying when their
mouths are full of sugar. Or when they're laying face
down in the street. Communication is all about failure,
but I'm all about secret messages. Made for tape. It's how
I'm not learning to get out of Los Angeles.

*

I bang on my neighbor's door but he refuses to let me in.
I hear children's voices. He says he's working on science
fiction.

*

I have been told that I'm a stoner. Also I've been told
that all the homeless people are really poets. Like art is a
kind of poverty. A homeless person told me I had a coca-
cola mouth. "Go home coca-cola mouth," he told me as I
passed him by. "But I am home," I pleaded.

*

The pool in the courtyard is hard to get out of.
I think about my body and I think about watching
footage from riots in Brazil.
Fashion can ruin the state as well as make the state more
powerful.

All these stadiums will burn like sugar.
I'm wrecking my collection of funeral candy because I'm
homesick.
Take me out of here, I whisper.
We are modern in a private way.

❄

Emily Dickinson.

❄

"Narrative: The narrative is a running, general-terms
description of the conditions of the crime scene. The
narrative describes the scene in a "general to specific"
reference scheme. Use a systematic approach in
narrative. Nothing is insignificant to record if it catches
one's attention. Under most circumstances, do not collect
evidence during the narrative. Use photographs and
sketches to supplement, not substitute, for a narrative.
The narrative should include case identifier; date, time,
and location; weather and lighting conditions; condition
and positions of the evidence."

❄

*A photograph to remember me by:* Let's not fool ourselves.
There are still scraps from the riots blowing around
the feet of our dinner table. We're eating lamb with

our make-up tools. It's the first meal after the riot. The loudspeakers are still burning. Most kings get their heads cut off at the opera.

✳

I have a mouth if you have a rag.

I have a body if you have a riot.

Scrapie, scrapie you can't catch me.

✳

Nicanor, when you finally die, I will use pig grease to make something beautiful out of your ribcage, something like a monument. The rest I'll donate to fashion.

✳

I keep thinking about the word "Aquamarine."

✳

The only thing I really have left from the cold war is a bracelet and I'm using it to measure my son's wrists. When I was his age I was carried through hospital corridors in the arms of a nurse. Her name was Humiliation.

＊

My daughter loves Langston Hughes because he writes
about dreams, she says. What does she dream about?
Mostly hermit crabs and butterflies and colorful ponies
that can talk. She cries when I start to throw out the
oranges she's placed around the apartment to feed the
butterflies. I'm sick of the stench, of waking up to that
flutter around my sores and eyes. She is also complaining
about the pork.

＊

Bakers commonly refer to burning sugar as "liquid
napalm."

＊

While making marshmallows for my daughters I spilled
sugar syrup on my hand (pinky finger) and arm. Since
it didn't really hurt my arm, I attended to my finger first
and ignored the splatter. Ran cold water on my pinky
and then peeled the syrup off my arm. I've put an ice
pack on my hand to prevent blistering.

＊

Sugar doesn't melt, it decomposes.

＊

A huge explosion and fire occurred at the Imperial
Sugar Refinery north of Los Angeles, causing 14 deaths
and injuring 38 others, including 14 with serious and
life-threatening burns. The explosion was fueled by a
massive accumulation of combustible sugar dust through
the packaging building. The aluminum cover meant
to keep out contamination allowed the sugar dust to
accumulate to an explosive concentration.

＊

The man next door pretends he's working on a safer
design for sugar refineries but he's not answering the
door and I still hear the pitter-patter of little feet. Once
he told me that he had come to Los Angeles because he
thought all his dreams would come true here. A prospect
horrifying and reminiscent of colonialism. But I came
here for the same reason, and I've accumulated bodies as
well. Last night I dreamt about a machine that would get
rid of all bodies. It was a breathing machine. From it, I
learned how to write poetry.

＊

Making sugar out of slaves

Spunk

Silver fluency

Sometimes I can't be bothered to make sentences

Lethe-wards

The trope of the diabetic narrative

❋

I signed a contract with sloppy ink and I couldn't tell
what the whole thing said only that I did sign it and I
wore a bracelet when I signed it when I signed it I didn't
plagiarize my signature I plagiarized the bracelet and I
signed the bracelet but it was plagiarized and I signed
it too by putting out my cigarette on my arm but in so
doing I was just full of hate. I'm sorry, I couldn't help it.

❋

RIP Frank Lima

❋

RIP Wanda Coleman

❋

I'm drawing a picture of my son but the mosquitoes get in the way and outside Los Angeles seems to be burning again. The teen angels are messing with lanterns. I'm scared that my son will become famous. I fear he will return in stained furs and thousands of bodies will belong in his fame.

❀

If the scrapie agent was a virus, it was different from every other known virus. Sheep, like people, have elaborate immune systems for recognizing and destroying foreign protein such as the protein coats of viruses – but like kuru, scrapie caused no inflammation, raised no fevers, evoked no immune response at all.

❀

Quicksilver
Mercury
Slow explosion of metal
Cunt
The trigger

❀

Last night I lay around thinking about numbers – the sublime nature of numbers – how car crashes make us modern – how corpses make a president powerful – how anti war protestors love numbers just as much. Count

backwards, swan around los-angeles-soft in a dead
person's suit. Count backwards. Start with 1.

*

Today I came upon a young prostitute in the colorful
glare of oriental lanterns. She told me something that
was so terrible that I could not tell my daughters, could
not even tell my wife. I had to tell it to my son, thinking
his purity would protect him. You cannot destroy Los
Angeles, I explained to him. I have tried with this love
poem and it has only made things worse.

THE GOD TO WHOM I CONFESS IS AN
EXPERT ADMINISTRATOR

Sometimes I have a bleeding heart but sometimes I don't
because I listen to the music of Los Angeles
the sound of pigs being concussed on slaughterhouse floors
the sound of teenagers with a thin
layer of pubic hair over everything
and sometimes if you listen hard enough in Los Angeles
you can hear an interrogation taking place in Los Angeles
or you can hear Capital
or you can hear a deer get shot in the head
while poets want me to say something cute and crazy
about wanting to stay in bed
I stay in bed if my wife is in bed because she has big tits
and then I go to an opening
which is a beautiful lie (the only kind worth dying for).
It was torn down last night because
a janitor thought it was trash. So it's a lie.
It's also about homosexual desire.
And black-on-black violence. Violence-on-violence violence.
Like your show, Los Angeles.
Like my show, Ruins, your show is all about like
sleepwalking and shit. Like my show, your hype comes out
of epilepsy and social media.
We fuck with slurred mouths.
I'm always singing about Mexico, always singing about
swan and radios
on the operating table with this fucked up voice.
When is your show taking place?
Tonight at the abortion clinic.
Tonight in New Jerusalem.

Tonight I'll walk into a bar for authors and order a bullet
in the head.
When in Rome
when all else fails
imitate the natives with dead flowers.
Wake up in the middle of the night and ask for a
thrashing fox.
Pig out

On our way home at night, my wife and I walk through a street where whores stroll and strut. They have a beautiful perfume, or many perfumes that blend together beautifully. Some of them are beautiful and that makes us happy. Some of them are too young and look beaten-up and this makes us sad. One night there's a slight rain and it makes us all somewhat moist, makes us feel as if we and the prostitutes were in collusion. One young woman grabs me tenderly around my waist and says, "Can you take me with you?" We look at her. She is beautiful but kind of disfigured. We say sure, and we take her with us. I think: in a few weeks, she will suck black milk.

Fucked in… this like… swarm of butterflies
we thought was maybe stenciled out
of some horrible movie about transcendence but we couldn't
prove it we could only name bodies and then Romanticism
came back with its body (leaves, snow, media).
I don't want to read a poem
unless it tells me where the killer hides… I kind of want him
to invite me into his ruins. I want him to be like… a whore.
The whore we brought with us to the motel is named Desire.
She was a victim of Art. She looked like a prostitute so
she was one. She had become a favorite of the military
occupation.

# EKPHRASIS/COCAINE

I am so skinny I am beautiful like a rape field.
But my style is not sustainable, according to the whores,
because I can hardly breathe when I read poetry out loud
or when I'm hanging like a lantern from their rape tree.
What do you know about sustainable, I should tell the
whores, you who powder your wigs with arsenic and wear
mercury on your lips just to make your kisses tingle?
But I don't tell them that. I'm too busy starving.
Too busy stealing rifles inlaid with
silver and bone fragments.
Sara tells me about stealing drugs
to shoot up in a hotel room much like ours.
Surveillance cameras make me want to go anorexic.
I have such beautiful hair in grainy cinema. Sometimes
people assume I'm a homosexual because I look good
when I interrogate prisoners.
I have petals in my mouth.
The instruments look allegorical in Los Angeles.
Even the parrot's perch means something. My dripping
mask is going to hell with insects. The whole thing getting
disarticulated up by nature... And it smells bad.
Especially in this mouthpiece.
There are definitely petals in my mouth now that I think
about it, they must be there because I hate evidence and I
hate to wear Disney masks on my crotch.
– What?
No, I won't rip the tape off.

Someone might accuse me of trying to hide my blood money.
It's not true, I'm writing this on blood money.
Sara is using blood money to finance
her recreations of Francesca Woodman's mansion.
I gave blood money to her
because I can't stop thinking about Francesca Woodman.
What will you wear, I ask her solemnly.
My husband's blood, she replies.
What drugs will you use, I ask her solemnly.
My husband's blood, she replies.
She's fastening something that looks like a hook in the
ceiling. She must have bought it from the slaughterhouse in
the heart of glamour. I saw it there. I too wanted to be torn
apart there.

Luxurie: One person is the subject and the other the object.
My daughters: I have poked holes in the trinkets.
Plague: You said sleep was like fighting with dogs.
Rapture: You said sleep was like fighting with dogs.
Consumption: I said I wanted to get hyped up.
Kitsch: I said I wanted to rule you absolutely.
Sensation: You wanted to rule me like furious eyelashes.

Are you dancing with him in this one or did you do that to his forehead? I ask Sara about her Francesca Woodman remakes. It's a little hard to tell because the surveillance footage is so grainy, Sara admits.

Also, you don't really look like Francesca Woodman, I tell her. Please, careful! I tell her as she inserts the needle in my arm. Please! I yell.

I understand that she's going for a surveillance aesthetic, and I too find staring at people like that beautiful, but she might be going too far. That's all I'm saying. And I'm also saying, just because Francesca Woodman shaved her pussy doesn't mean you have to.

No, I'm not shaving my pussy, I tell her.

Sara is working with her husband, the photographer.
He's debased, he went to the Congo and barely returned.
He returned with these skulls that he gave me as a
wedding gift. He married me to the nightmare of the
black body, the innocence riots. The hooves.
When he held up "the mother cake", I said no no no, I'm
already married, I've already married and my wedding
gift was ground meat.
Sara is melting something colorful in her spoon.
My wife is covered in snow, it's melting. I won't let Sara
near her because today she's happy. My wife wants to
fuck, but her language is fucked up.
I do things to her "fitta."

*I have a fever:* A young Asian woman – utterly without plastic or pubic hair – has brought me an old-fashioned phonograph, on which she plays an old standard about the moraine fish. The woman has a high-pitched voice. She opens her hand: insect antennae. I can feel blood trickling down my lips I can hear a crunch. I am too weak to spit…

Sinéad asks me if cats eat bats or bats eat cats. I don't
know, I reply. Go ask your mother. But her mother
is busy examining a colorful coral reef flourette,
cutting into its soft skin with her gilded scalpel. Some
neighborhood whores gave it to my wife to thank her for
performing abortions in our bathroom. There's a little
inscription from a song on the handle: "Life imitates Art."

We shouldn't trust metaphors I've been told.
The girl is not a plague, the hare is not poetry, the threat is
not nuclear, the war is not the war.
I'm partying on the war.
I'm picking up on its mysticism.

Sara needs more sugar for her photographs.
She wants to shoot in the slaughterhouse.
I can't pork anymore
not since Baghdad fell not since the green zone
I get so greasy and my wife might be pregnant again
I haven't eaten for days
Eurydice, can we live in a nation of animal bodies
can we live
with all these mirrors and Hong Kongs
Can I be a great hunter
Can I sleep in the snow
I am too weak to even hold the revolver up
to hold the silkscreen up to the light
to get rid of the flies around my daughter's eyes
I'm getting fat
I'm myself but I'm also underground
also more than myself and less than a puppet
in a game that smells like meat
and the Lust Garden of Suffering is another name
for the allegory I suffer through
The story of joy
the ampules are open
the street is foggy
The children are Japanese
I have to pull my wife out of the underworld
I have to nail her against the wall

I have a fever with an asian girl utterly without
plastic or pubic hair
I am too weak to spit
I can feel the blood trickling down my chin
My wife walks to the window which glows
She's eating a nectarine
I finally have father death in a souvenir store

My daughter: "The heat, pappa, is killing us!"

Today my wife carved up a rat brain, placed it
on the glass pane, and looked at it through her microscope.
Today I think about the mouths we stuffed
in the movie about police violence.
I think about the horrific close-ups
and they reminded me of when I was "satanic"
for a few hours.
Tomorrow I will find no leads so I'll bust up
that mannequin in my living room. I'll fill it
with sand and pubic hair.
I'll use my cigarette lighter to melt the skin.
My daughters will be horrified
because they call it "Mother."
It's a male mannequin though, so I don't know
why that would be. Perhaps because it has no
penis but it doesn't have a vagina either.
Perhaps that's why I have to burn it.

## GANG BANG

I'm also embedded but I feel lonely today
because my wife and children are gone.
I burn easily. Once I had a girlfriend who liked to
collect my sperm in a glass ampule.
I can't tell the difference anymore
between mass graves and Duchamp.
I think everything is made of pig.
A swimming pool made of pig meat: Baghdad.
Every great work of art is made of pig.
I can't tell the difference between
great works of art and murder trials.
There are so many beautiful legs in this city
and that makes me want to fuck but I keep writing
because I'm hungry and thirsty and I keep seeing
a portrait of the artist as a corpse on a mirror.
Pig corpse on a cracked mirror.
I watch the movie about hunger strikes again.
I remember how afterward my body was "placed in the frost."

"Put down your fire arms,
put down your pet arms,
put down your cameras,
put down your animals,
put down your novels,
put down your children,
put down your children's children,
put down your party favors,
put down your bright red shirts
put down your over-written books,
put down your areolas,
put down your funny hats,
put down your down payments... etc "

I have this busted radio
that I like to whistle into.
My sleep sparkles.
Like a poster for an auction house.
Like I'm skinny again with skin.
And red with terrorists.
I'm watching them on TV
doing their collage thing
in the mall. Dazzling bodies,
widow bodies, inviting the
cameras into their cocaine.
Those bodies can still be traded
in at the auction house.

"Who did this to you," asks my wife when she's removed the tape.

"God," says my daughter and laughs.

"Los Angeles," says my wife and laughs.

# I HAVE MY WAR PAINT AND I'M AUTISTIC WHEN I'M ALIVE

I wake up thinking about porcelain and sounds
from that hotel room
where the starlet and I made many mistakes
when we depicted war bodies.
My wife is almost dead from mercury poisoning
and sits in the sofa counting "pigs."
The most burning thing in the world is a beehive (my
father burned the hives when we moved because he
didn't want anybody else to tend to them, he locked the
bees inside and he still smells like gasoline even though
he's dead).
The most famous person in the world is Hitler.
I can hear a recording from the neighbor's room
but it seems slower than usual... like the tape is dragging.
Sara doesn't want to do drugs anymore
but she is very detailed in her plans for our bodies.
It's like cross-stitching that goes bad. Her husband has been
fucking women in the Congo as part of a film he's doing.
It sounds like imagery from my heart of darkness.
Another image from my heart of darkness shows a man
screaming in a hut.
The Americans giggle. Americans are always giggling.
Americans giggle all the time because they don't hate
anything except hatred.
And I hate them right back.

A madwoman haunts our street. She swears at prostitutes and begs for money. She has a child wrapped in cloth. We never see the child because it's completely covered in cloth. We suspect it's not a real child but a prop to help her beg for food. Still, we give her money now and then. The prop works. Until one day she is out there yammering, "I don't want to have this child anymore. I can't take care of this child anymore. My last child is buried in the park, and I don't want this one to die." It's very dramatic. She walks up to us and says "Please, take my child." We don't know what to do. We ask, "Is it sick?" "No, but it won't survive much longer," yells the mad woman and opens up the gauze. It is a real child. But it's dead. "It's dead," I say. "No it's not, it's just sleeping!" she shouts and starts to poke the child's body with her fingers. "It's done this before," she explains. But it doesn't move. It doesn't start to breathe. "You've killed my child!" she screams and falls down on her knees. "Please, you must seek help," I try. "And who would help me?" she laughs and spits at our feet. She bends over her child again and cries. "I curse you," she gasps in her tears. "I curse you to give birth to child after child. I curse you to so many children a whole army wouldn't be able to kill them all!" We leave her there, cursing us over her dead child.

Did I ever note that we have a sun room? We have a sun room but it reeks of sperm. I don't even like to fuck in there.

(The only music I hear in this city is girls. The only posters I see advertise medicine that may cause damage to your cornea. The opium-blue hue makes me think that the wars are being used to sell art. I feel like a war prop. I have a war prop. A thrash-media. I pose next to a drill. I pose next to a credit card. I am naked while a shrine is infiltrated. I have a drill next to my head. I have an autopsy. I have been billed as an inmate but I am more alarmed. I have a more underwater look on my face when I say cheese. I scream cheese. I feel the cheese dripping down my chin. I feel like a war prop. I want pork. I want pork in the swimming pool. I want to pork you up. I want the victims to reproduce the original crime. I want the ecstasy of the third world to be realized when I am posed next to girl bodies. I feel like a war prop. I have a war prop in my mouth. The cunts of celebrities have been covered up. The cunts of the soldiers have been covered up. Mouths talk about a war. They sound like they're being gagged. I have a war prop. I want a war prop.)

## LINEAGE THAT GOES WRONG AND THEN WE BEGIN THE VOMIT

My daughter is not me. She doesn't fuck homeless people
and she doesn't want to watch *The Reign of Terror* again.
She's stuck with a counterfeit daddy who stinks like rotting
oranges and drinks like a holocaust dummy.
But I'm not on film, I'm on cocaine.
I'm on the cooling boards and I want a reservation blanket
and a slaughterhouse for fun. When I leave my daughters
it's like leaving a crash-course in virginity. It's a gross
understatement to say I want to make my poems more like
snuff films but what does that mean? Does it mean I want
the real thing in art or art as a replacement for the real
thing? Which one is worse? I'll take that one.
I can't stop cumming on my wife's silk outfits.
I can't stop fucking homeless people to
get them to shut up about their dead babies.
You should have put some fucking food in your baby's mouth!
... I can't stop thinking about her dead baby.
I can't stop remembering Yideum giving me a fox stole to
wear to the press conference. The room smelled like squid.
It was media. It was Los Angeles is beautiful because the
utter consumption ruins ever subject position. It's like...
I admire her cast very much....Her soundtrack is pure
sugar... Pop music like we get knocked out in a field of
poppies... Rape poppies.
I want to make a screwy dolls for every hot chick who
has died in that field with her mouth all berry-stained and
beautiful.

I want the doll to be adolescent and used to supplant real women for the industry. Yuck. My son thinks that's funny. Sometimes I forget to feed my son for several days and then I need to brush some sugar on his lips to bring him back. But my wife is too far gone
for just a little sugar.
I have to fuck her in the mouth.

The bees are becoming extinct.
They are turning black like black cocaine or black milk.
Even the whores are turning black.
Whores are beautiful in Los Angeles
and I take their photographs: cadavers for the allegory.
– Crime does not pay.
I can't tell what the person on the security camera is doing
to the other person.
A dance of sorts. The Twist. The Crawl.
The perpetrator looks like me but more disheveled,
more fucked.
The victim looks like a virgin if you know what I mean.
20,000 leagues beneath the sea: if you know what I mean.
When I adopt the right pose I too look like a virgin
but I also look like I'm with child.
With war.

JOURNAL OF A PLAGUE YEAR

My wife is depressed. The children are killing her. I have a photograph of the children painting their faces with resin and shark-blood and they are smiling and in the background my wife sits exhausted with swollen eyes. She can't take their cackling anymore. A dark blotch has started to take shape in her. Like a photograph or a bleed-through: Now she is sitting in the swimming pool, which is empty except for photographs and rat poison. Now she's writing a play about crime. She wants it to take over. Burn Los Angeles down. Burn it all down to cinders. But don't start over. Never start over. Continue to burn: that is all art can do now that our bodies have been made into posters, our love into The Law.

It has also been observed with great uneasiness by People that the weekly Bills in general have increased over the past few weeks although it is during the time when bills are much more moderate. The most recent bill is especially scary, being a higher number than what had been buried in one week during the last visitation of the plague in the late 1980s.

Some people want to round up the homeless
or return to the gold standard.
I get it: I want to write a book about the holocaust.
But it will be just one more book about skin and shoes.
The body is always involved, but only as decoy.
Whores are incredible. It breaks my heart. This party
among statues.
Sara says: Nobody shot in the head, no party.
According to her, the road to joy is lined with photographs.
In each photograph Sara is cradling a "baby deer."
The plague makes images of the body.
The bovine outbreak was first captured on video.
That's why I have to buy a new suit. It's like I have to
drown myself in silk.
I have to burn myself with cigarettes. I have to be beaten
to death by cops.
Every day is suffering. Buddhism taught me that.
Life is not realistic.
Art taught me that. It's not even life.
The Iraq War taught me that.

Today I give some candy to a prostitute even though I know her pussy is shaven and I ask her why she has that nasty bruise on her face. It makes her face look almost purple. She won't tell me. Her boyfriend went to Vietnam and he's dead. She tells me to go to Hell. Los Angeles is not Hell. If it was hell there would be no sperm in her snatch and no liver in my mouth. She spits it in my face. Recordings can still sound too slow and tapes can still melt if they are thrown into a burning barn and maybe pigs will trample on it first or eat it like how they eat the ears off children. I'm not an animal. I'm not an animal. Yes, you are.

I'm not naked by the door but I have had it with
all this "cutting to the bone" rhetoric in poetry.
Insects are alive and history is never over.
Once I had a friend who had a tiny penis inside her cunt;
it dribbled milk and blood.
After a gang-bang, my body was wrapped in gauze.
When my wife stuffs me with cake
I just lay back in the bathtub.
The charcoal is meant to bring me back to life.
The meat is meant to make me puke.
The hallucinations are meant to be exit wounds.
Of all the synonyms for "son," I think "Art" best captures
the drained, emptied sense of it. The trees look like
paper. The coffins look like porcelain...
It smells like burning plastic but I cum in my wife's pussy.
Then we lay in the bed and smell the plastic.
I remember the pop song "Overture to the Naked Stag
of My Hanging," which I used to hum when I was sad.
Since that time, I have found out what people mean
when they say La la la.
The material is *crêpe* de chine.

I check my son for signs of the Disease. He refuses to comply so I put a hood over his head and ask him questions he can't understand. Bingo.

There's a craze for aquariums in Los Angeles. Sometimes people fill them with colorful fish or vicious fish, and sometimes with stuff from nature (Ferns, worms, rotting meat). Or they just keep the aquariums empty. Or they keep their pets in them. But mostly they use the aquariums for colorful fish and anemone. Sometimes the truly beautiful Los Angeles inhabitants will sniff cocaine off shards of aquariums or bury their children in gilded aquariums.

My daughter has red rings around her ankles. I believe these to be Tokens of the Disease, but my wife believes she has merely been bitten by a snake. Our servants left. They'd had enough. However, days later they were found in the desert, including their 6-year-old daughter. They simply did not prepare for the long journey.

*Katrina-Sade (2009):* News is spreading about nurses giving patients radical new forms of treatment for the Plague. One apparently put a wet cloth upon the face of a dying patient who she attended, and so put an End to his Life, who was just expiring before. And another that smothered a young woman she was looking to, when she was in a fainting fit and would have come to herself. Some killed patients by giving them one Thing, some Another, and some starved them by giving them nothing at all.

I hate evidence.
I can still barely read because of the rat poison.
We should go to a masquerade with
my wife and her mercury lips.
The room in which Sara is re-envisioning
Francesca Woodman with fake blood on her tits
is so decked out with toys it's kind of scary.
I'm in one photograph with nose-blood.
I look so white it's like I'm fainting. It's like, I'm beautiful.
It's hard to capture the texture of plastic bags
unless they are filled with hair.
It's hard to know what she wants me to do
since she won't tell me straight out.
She starts telling me about shooting
horses in Los Angeles.
It's disgusting to be covered in paper cranes.
This story is disgusting because we are in Los Angeles
looking for a killer and killers are bred by art, which is
disgusting when you think about it. All that raw burger
meat. All that bloody mess in plastic bags.

POEM THAT NEEDS TO BE PROCESSED:

Snow flickers through the air.
It brings victims to our backyard.

*Scene from the film* Revolver: Bessie Smith lies down in the snow next to the tsar's little bleeder. A man looks at them from a window. It's a large window. There are several scores in the window frame. One of the panes are broken. The wind rushes in. The man tries to nail some plywood to cover it up but his fingers are so cold. This scene, found on the cutting-room floor, is dedicated to Eva Braun.

*(For James Pate)*

Sometimes Heaps and Throngs of People would burst out of that Alley, most of them Women, making a dreadful Clamour, mixt or Compounded of Skreetches, Cryings and Calling one another, that we could not conceive what to make of it; almost all the dead Part of the Night the dead Cart stood at the End of that Alley, for if it went in it could not well turn again, and could go in but a little Way. There, I say, it stood to receive dead Bodys, and as the Church-Yard was but a little Way off, if it went away full it would soon be back again: It is impossible to describe the most horrible Cries and Noise the poor People would make at their bringing the dead Bodies of their Children and Friends out to the Cart, and by the Number one would have though, there had been none left behind, or that there were People enough for a small City liveing in those Places: Several times they cryed Murther, sometimes Fire: but it was esie to perceive it was all Distraction, and the Complaints of Distress'd and distemper'd People.

When I ask Sara how to tell if I have the plague, she tells me to breathe on a mirror. If I have the plague we will see writhing little creatures on the glass. I don't see any.

My wife tells me that our daughters have started spitting back up the food she's feeding them. They're upset because they watched a movie in which a puppy disappeared into jello. They think the puppy is dead even though in the movie it came back and saved the day. "I don' t know anything about dogs," my wife yells into the phone.

# I CUT UP THE FLOWERY KINGDOM FOR YOU

The scorpion wakes up every time I fuck my wife
like the movies
in Cairo.
We hate the oriental deaths prescribed by the Law of Joy
but we love the aftermath.
I love the whores who teach us
about cockroaches and electricity
and my wife loves the disarticulation of the body-symbolism.
I think Sara is making a new toy for her private eye.
I'll be the carcass on the mirror
if you will be the cattle bones.
I'm reading about Nazi aesthetics again and it makes me want
to starve and/or eat too much.
I say some stuff to nobody in particular about rotting fruit
and the girls in the disco who put rat poison in their cake
because they want their cake and they want to kill it too.
I want to kill it too.
I wonder if those girls would have liked my new
lampshade. My daughters have made it out of historical
artifacts so to speak.
Sara wants me to watch some porn because it's not porn,
it's teeming with marionettes. Who made this? She doesn't
know, she found it after a drive-by shooting.
While walking home I pretend I have the clap,
the kissing disease,
can exterminate this whole city with a kiss.

## THE CHILDREN OF PARADISE

This hotel might just collapse
because my wife and I are really siblings
and when we fuck we fuck with the white race.
We sniff cocaine with the white race
but we sniff it from Asian bodies.
Small-boned Asian bodies.
Degeneracy is something that happens to white people.
In their Art.
We're so fucking skinny when we're white
we sometimes go backwards and become homosexuals
or just choke in hotels. I'm so white, I'm your lover.
You're so white you're more beautiful than Nagasaki.
The murder was based on real bodies no doubt
but my immunity system didn't recognize the foreign
proteins. The riot was called The Deadly Feast.
My son says: I'm gonna get you with this mouth.
He has a Satanic Glow.
Like he wants to masturbate the walls.
Barbwire shadows on his face.
Silk is the most popular fabric in Los Angeles.
White is the color of love.

This morning on the official sign that read "This Area Is Under Surveillance" somebody had slapped a sticker that said "MY HEART IS A BOMB!"

# THE CONFERENCE OF BIRDS

## THE BEGINNING

There are so many laws wow in Los Angeles!
I love laws but I get thrown out of the museum!
Francesca Woodman wears mary-janes and I wear the
orpheus mask because then I can get torn into pieces
and I can tear her shit up.
She wears the bird mask from Iraq because then she will
almost be alive.
She can move around the ruins like in a video game
while my soul reminds us of drones or whores,
jacklightingly white.
Maybe I'll nail the posters around my room: her in
Afghanistan, her in the white house, me in the frost, after
the gang-bang.
In that picture my dick is like half-limp but I'm not
conscious. Seriously. I'm not for free and I'm not very
clean. Capitalism wants to humiliate us but we're too
busy eating history like cake.
If you look at me you will see that I am beautifully pale,
even now with my erection. In the shed. Please. I hate
everyone - it's why I wear silk.
I ask a beautiful whore where she gets her sugar.
She says it comes from thousands of miles away at
stunning speeds. It's the only thing that can cure the
plague, she claims.
It collapses the distinction between Luxurie and
Necessity.
She tastes like bubble gum in her pussy.

I taste like fois gras on my cock.
The bikinis look like moths from this angle - Am I stoned?
Am I a girl when I run into a museum of contemporary
art? There's an exhibition of media art and the media is
televisions screens not meat but the language is about meat
and the meat is about the war and the war tick-tick-ticks
meat. It says "Cannibalism." It says "Sweet joy." It says "I'm
ashamed of the rats." It says "Sounds." It skins me because
I'm a girl and have a war.
And all the soft animals look at me, but I've had enough of them.
I want to become a great hunter.
I'll use a feather to puke and I'll be surrounded by flowers.
Ruin porn, they'll call me to my face. Ruin porn, they'll
whisper behind my back. And that's just the beginning.

The hate laws are a lot like the love laws.
My wife wakes up and messes with the sugar she has a
hole in her hand and it snows outside when I speak to her
about the soul and the dark stuff glimmers.
Another thing: oriental death.
Also, the firing squads are not poetic any longer.
Sara is making a new toy, called the "ouch-ouch."
What does it do?
It's a kind of joy.

## MY ORPHEUS MASK IS SHITTY WHEN I FUCK FRANCESCA WOODMAN

I'm listening to that song about ball gowns that drip blood
and I think the singer is kind of cute. Kind of like one of
those saints that smell like sperm.
I think about masturbating on a masterpiece because I
want to see myself on surveillance footage.
I'm kind of writing this while a python rots in the ground.
Maybe if I dug it up it would be sensational....Danz musique...
I don't understand any of these laws but I know I have to
be the immigrant because there's a law against him.
His outfits are too beautiful or he has cuckoo-mouths.
I know that I am getting fantastically corseted
for the Finale.
When the Finale is over I might find my own killer in ruin
porn. Or actresses might find me enacting a threat with my
wax dolls and my body doubles and my cock which looks
like it's made of wax after sex.
I look like a virgin because I'm scared and I'm drinking
black milk from my wife's hands. From her Hiroshima glass.
Have you ever heard of an orpheus as stupid as me? My
cum is all black when I come back from the underworld
with my wife.
I look out the window and Los Angeles looks all kabuki
and the orphans are locked in. My wife smashes window
and that's her threat. Her ultra poetry. Her diary full of
hairstyles. Her fascist snow. Nobody can play the starlet

but everyone can play me. Everyone can touch the tsar's
little bleeder. It's free.
But you can't touch my wife.
I hate everyone.
I should keep my mouth shut
but it's too full and my lips are smeared with lipstick
manufactured by the dead women of Juarez.

# NOW I HAVE YOU IN THE UNDERWORLD

I'm trying to sing to my wife, trying to pay off Death
to keep him out of her snatch. I tell her about the pubic
hair of pigs and blood tsunamis but she won't open her
eyes. Los Angeles is crawling with lice, according to my
daughters. I comb their hair and look for lice but it's
hard to find them. They must be quick. I feel them in my
own body. The lice. On my daughter I find only evidence
in the form of eggs. I lay on the floor and the butterflies
land on my face. I want to be adored is the message. In
the street the whores are cutting each other's hair for the
hanging or to sell it or to get rid of the lice. What's the
matter with these bitches? These egregious bodies: they
want to blame the hair? What's in my mind tonight? I
don't know but in my heart of darkness I have abortions
and candy surrealism.

# I SUFFER FROM VERTIGO IN THE SEPULCHRAL CHAMBERS OF THE LAW

My proverbial son is staring at the bird in
that one little window in his room: it's porn.
It's how he'll be infected.
Everything is porn, says Sara while feeding
Chinese food to homeless people
in her latest video.
Sometimes I feel like I'm involved
in a desperate advertising campaign
trying to sell the 21$^{st}$ century.
All those prisoners and all that shaven pussy:
you'd think it would be an easy job.
Nothing is easy when you have to
deal in overexposed bodies.
I vomit a little from the sugar-high and then go
search for my daughters who are
playing with screwy dolls and millionaires.
I have to find a killer but I'm worried he
doesn't even know who I am.
Sinéad is all snotty in her face and screaming:
she must be throwing a tantrum.
She's plugged her hare into an electrical outlet.
Nobody listens. I'm putting down my arms.
Sometimes when I wear my orpheus mask
and my mouth is full of pomegranates
I want to remember my past,
but mostly I'm just sick or horny or I want to

shoot a bullet through my head: The story of Joy.
I have a landscape fetish
but only when it's made of naked bodies.
I make my paint out of women's cum and spit.
I make a language out of the bleed-through.
I describe my "pillow angel."
No doves survive and I have eating disorders.
Now I'm wearing my new shoes to the interrogation.

# SAFE IN MY CHAMBERS OF ALABASTER

Surveillance cameras make it hard to see what Sara is
doing to her crotch.
We're dying but we can't find any evidence.
Every time I make an image of myself an angel dies.
I'm shivering cold because I feel too much,
for example about my wife who has tits in Los Angeles.
My son asks me about a girl who shivers and doesn't
have eyes,
so I leave him and go to a media museum.
The topic is virgin violence.
I pretend to know my way around. I pretend to translate
images into words but if there's one thing I've learned
about translation: it's about corpses.
Dig me up in a 100 years and I'll tell you about children
dying outside my window. How they smelled like rotten
fruit. So what.
Tonight whores are going to sew in my dolls.
There's a worm in my hand and it's small and white.
It comes from the flowers some whores gave me last
night while I was walking home with my white face and
shaking hands.
The media museum smells bad it reminds me of the
whores' gowns and how they burned.
My son is frantically beating on the wall.
He's scared whores will burn the house down.
They won't, whore-boy.

Japanese Linden
True Lice
Kallimini
Locust leaf miner
Locust bush
orchid mantid
lupine

My son is poster material
is fois gras is cannibalism is "sounds ok" is puking silk.
My son has the most open mouth in Los Angeles of Ugly.
I'm "sick" and a "shut-in" I suppose. I keep thinking,
"noctuid" because of the sci-fi angle. The bomb angle. The
multiply-killed-wife angle. The rich flower angle.
The shutting of houses: It seems to have opened my house up.
It seems to have
Punched me in the spine.
Wow so stoned it's like meat and bikinis.
An island swoon kind of. The illustrations say you are evil
and "rape fields."
Silver poetry, silver males...A mouth full, right?
My son has turned allegorical on surveillance footage or
else he used to be allegorical and now his image is too
thick... It suddenly happens that I'm fainting out aloud in
a bomb-like atmosphere.
When I come back I'm teasing my daughters about prisoners.
My son maybe is the child of reason... The reason we
kill the genius child... My wife's mercury levels are also
beautiful but harmful... Anti-abortion protestors are
beautiful except that they want to kill.
There are mumble bodies... I understand the logic... No
more poetry... No more darlings to kill...
My wife is glorious today, it's like she could be the new Los
Angeles, sweeping up the dead butterflies... tossing out rotten
fruit... My wife is glorious but she doesn't know the difference
between word and world. The difference is son.

No, I'm not that shy./I've never seen my wife cry. Is it too late to say I think Los Angeles is the most beautiful city in the world? I have no defenses in this city because my skin is for shit. The orient is for wigs. I belong in the shooting range with the other bodies./Berlin/Things are much better in the underworld, I've heard on the radio. The dream radio, scream radio, rat radio./I have to be beaten by cops, you spumey fuck./"Behind every tree, a sharpshooter" they used to joke in Kosovo. Behind every whore a different language, I joke at the Faust-party. I am always joking. / An interrogator looks at me and asks me to write down this confession.

My wife tells me to lie still. Lie still, she shouts.
My wife wants to wear a snow-colored necklace when
she puts me back together again but she also wants to
read to me from her book of atrocity fashion. The sperm
is dribbling out of her cunt. I want to read *Merchant
of Venice* for the meat imagery. I want to be a Riding
Instructor for meat imagery.
My wife tells me about a book she's read in which a
distant planet makes every man's dreams come true. I say
how beautiful, but she says no it's horrible, lots of pitter-
patter of children's feet, lots of naked black women.
Apparently one character keeps killing his wife.
Apparently she asks: why do you want to get rid of me?
She wasn't a virgin, I think. Media makes duplicates.
The planet was maybe media maybe a stand-in for Los
Angeles which is a stand in for cunts.
My wife's cunt is dripping sperm on the floor as she
walks to the window.
She will play Eva Braun in my next picture show.
My next picture will also feature scuffed mannequins
and rotten oranges because my daughters carry them
into the house to attract butterflies.
Butterflies swarm around my sore and my wife's cunt.
The enemy is a fake because he makes copies.
He will kill himself on Television.
My wife tells me that the road to joy is littered with
corpses.I think they have sperm on them.
She thinks they have Xs on them.

# COME WINTER AND KILL US ALL DEAD

I want aquariums to come back into style and I want
mine to be covered in black garbage bags
and then I want to sniff cocaine from the splinters.
I wish my son would just go to sleep and quit moaning.
I hope my daughters won't die until I have died though I
know I'm being morbid.
I've never taken voice lessons!
I must have a 100 degree fever because my sleep seems
to sparkle.
All the dazzling bodies in the street are so beautiful
I want to put them in Francesca Woodman's ruins.
I want to fuck Francesca Woodman in the snow: We'll be
the whitest art in the war against terrorism.
Hey I have a boner as I write this.
Hey I could live in an auction house if I could trade in
my own body instead of all those black bodies.
I have a breed poster in my room, it's a hate-breeding
poster. Architecture is meant to make us all porny but
what about Romanticism's deadly crime-flowers?
Can I sleepwalk through.
Can I sleepwalk through.
The bodies at the auction house: they belong to my
winter. The flies in my daughter's eyes belong to the
static air. The winter is sending messages to me it says I
can slaughter you you have no pubic hair don't burn me
down we don't have any plastic stuff on.

# MY SPERM GETS IN THE FLOWERS

I woke up from the girls tearing apart orpheus dolls and
spitting seeds out the window. Prostitutes cheered.
Now I'm wearing my orpheus head like an illicit sign
from the underworld.
Whores think I'm a pornographer and that I would tear
their heads off.
I probably would.
What's the war with my wife and me? We lay killed-like
in our den, our bodies covered with sugar and sperm.
Who are we at war with? Baghdad, of course.
Baghdad of silk and ceremonial daggers.
Baghdad dolls with limbs and heads that burn safely.
Baghdad porn: We watch it until we vomit and then we
watch it some more. We're embedded in art. We close
our eyes and let blue light wash over us.
Everybody is always talking about "gratuitous violence"
and "gratuitous sex."
It's like when people say "Porn hurts everyone" ... But
most of all I'm eating another dripping burger.
Flowers are violent props.
The Starlet would not have approved of us killing
butterflies with cigarette lighters.
It's Christmas Eve.
I'm writing a novel, my wife is listening for
"peonies" and "lilies" on broadcasts from the underworld.
Instead the broadcasts tell us that the birds are
"thrashing around the hole." It's of course Hollywood

speaking in tongues. Mother tongues tell me to name our
next child Nico after the underworld. After Baghdad.
After our favorite actress who is totally shaven.
Maybe we consume by looking but if so, consumption is
a very fragile thing.
I color my hair red as blood.
I cover the street with dead girls.
They are all ready for war.
I'm already famous.

There is a hair color for hatred.
There is a hair color for birth.
There is a hair color that is white.
There is a hair color that is ash.
There is a hair color that is Juarez.
There is a hair color that is bacteria.
There is a hair color that is things.
There is a hair color that is blind.
There is a hair color that is drained.
There is a hair color that is drown.
There is a hair color that is afternoon.
There is a hair color that is out.
There is a hair color that is in.
There is a hair color that is a hare color.
There is a hair color that is meat.
There is a hair color that is ant.
There is a hair color for finding the gun.
There is a hair color that is gun.
There is a hair color that is not.

We have to run after the children.
We can't lose them.
We have to run after them.
They are scared.
They are scared.
Their hair is the color of wheat.

Like a virgin in a pig-burial, I can't protest any longer.
I give up on ra-ta-ta.
I give up on a leaner, healthier, thrashier body.
I give up on infant death.
I give up on the theatrical enemy.
I give up on ding-dong dancing.
I just want to live in Samarkand and eat pussy.
The guns are pointing toward my nativity scene but I'm
already punctured.
The guns are pointing toward my children but I'm not there.
Everyone wants to do the jive with their hands tied behind
my back but I can't even bother to light a match anymore.
The pigs are eating gold out of my skull and I'm down on
my knees.
Some people claim they've seen me doing stupid shit with
my proverbial son and his bullet wounds. Other say I'm
doing the horsie-porsie with stupid prisoners.
I'm pounding out the confessions with a pound of flesh
shimmering on my desk. With a head full of pussy
and a mouth full of pussy and my game all gone in the
megaphones.
I will use duct tape and gashes to explain why my smile is
infectious. Now I'm explaining pictures. I'm the future of
awesome because I can't speak straight. Can't even walk
the road to joy without going all ching-ching.

I write about spectators and use the same rifle on sick animals.
I love movies and my son's body ticks because it is cold in here.
I have a fever in the movies probably.
A woman gives me a scorpion and children give me sickness.
I really only live at night, I've been told by the movies,
which is ridiculous because I use my hands to make the signs:
wrecks, chandeliers, hotels, decades, ownership society.
It's ridiculous because nobody can drive a stake through a
sack of locusts.
Part of me wants to be paid for the meat but part of me
wants to give it away like a whore.
The whores wear oriental robes, it's all the rage.
Everyone is angry in the movies.
Everyone is scared in corridors.
I tell my son to stop ticking but he can't hear me because
the whores are laughing too loudly and the plague makes
tokens of itself.
I love movies and perfume.
It's the new double, made from tiger blood.
It's the new breakthrough, made from tiger blood.
Milk is the weirdest when you're having sex.
I'm having a milk heart and that's why I can't watch movies
without getting scared. The milk gets all over. The deer gets
all narrative.
I turn on surveillance, turn on heat.
The effect is ominous: the reverse wound.
I look horrified in the image and also "satanic" due to the milk.
You spumey fuck.

*Ekphrasis*: A harlequin jewel bug guarding eggs on a stem. The highly modified head of bark beetle female showing hollowed head in which eggs are putatively carried and enlarged forceps-like antennae for picking up eggs and young.

*Ekphrasis:* The fashion brand Sleepwalker has made a line of mascara inspired by the women that line the streets of Los Angeles. The different colors are eyelids (charcoal), the stare (red), the ribcage (blue), the stumble (brownish). There is another line that compares women workers waiting for the bus to dummies. It's also inspired by Los Angeles.

Trumpets:

Children are hiding in the flowering tree (scared).
More children are hiding in the flowering tree (scared).
More children are hiding in the flowering tree (scared).
More children are hiding in the flowering tree (scared).
More children are hiding in the flowering tree (scared).
More children are hiding in the flowering tree (scared).
More children are hiding in the flowering tree (scared).
More children are hiding in the flowering tree (scared).
More children are hiding in the flowering tree (scared).
More children are hiding in the flowering tree (scared).
More children are hiding in the flowering tree (scared).
More children are hiding in the flowering tree (scared).
More children are hiding in the flowering tree (scared).
More children are hiding in the flowering tree (scared).
More children are hiding in the flowering tree (scared).
More children are hiding in the flowering tree (scared).
More children are hiding in the flowering tree (scared).
More children are hiding in the flowering tree (scared).

They have sperm on them that must be from the tree.
They have sperm on them that must be from The Law.

Every time the thrashing bodies ruin the map, I mean the poem that is Los Angeles burning down, but Los Angeles burns down, it's what it does. I'm just trying to get it to burn me down with it. I attended the riots but nothing happened. I wanted to steal a television for the camera but I looked too rich in my velvet coat, even though my sweater was yellow from puke and I smelled sour. Art is a luxury in America and Los Angeles is a symbol. Burning down Los Angeles is a luxurious act. Watching the horses get massacred or Lolita get sick and die in childbirth is even worse. It's porn. It's sugar. When my mouth is full of sugar I think of poor people. I think of cake. I think of violence. I write messages in blood on refrigerators. Silly goose.

I have begun to speak back to images because I'm tired of them speaking to me: Little girl go home.

# LOVE POEM WITH WHITE

I'll draw you in
to the picture where I'm
shadowing you
unshadowing you
I'm getting you back from the catacombs
the underground cinema
the emergency exit
the exit wound
where the light is reversed
I snuff it out with mercury
I have glass plaster and traffic for you
but I look anorexic without you
I will let you drive
will hype death like fever-lilies
chalk you out of the dark
with this poem
will play police and thief
with your body with your darkness
that I will chalk out
scrape away champagne you
I will kidnap your body out
of the winter palace
will shoot the faces off
the statues and slash up all
the paintings will climb you
out will seed the light for you

I will not look
will not look
will let Los Angeles tear me apart
play rabies with my body play horse-
scream with my mouth will play
hostage with my poetry
on its plague heaps with plastic bags
and I will play plague heaps
with plastic bags
will ruin my translation with plastic bags
carry sparrows by the thousands for you
in plastic bags and take you back
from the underground
to the overground
to the rotting shining mansions on the hill
where the water leaks
and the children are obnoxious
but I'll keep them safe for you
I'll carry them into the crash clear morning
sabotage

The girls are playing with splinters in the corner. The splinters used to be a mirror they used with their dolls. But they have disfigured the dolls and broken the mirror. They want to pour water on all of it but I say No. I don't want water everywhere. The radio is playing dance music, which my children love. There is a serial killer on the loose in Baghdad. These are all luxuries.

Tuinal
Yamamoto
Levinas
Chet Baker
Calvin Klein
Gerry Mulligan
Henry Parland
Deximal
Nembutal
Robert Mapplethorpe
Lithium
Duchamp
Stan Getz
Tarkovskij
Guy Debord
Zegna
Lars Norén
Stagnelius
Stagnelius
Stagnelius
Stagnelius
Rotten Leaves
Stagnelius
Andy Warhol
Race Riots
Electric Chair
Car Crash
Crash

Balloon in the Wires
Peer Gynt
Berlin
Los Angeles
Noir

One of our daughters has a funny eye. "The funny eye" we call it. But she calls it "the way to paradise." It's hard to figure out where she's getting paradise from because we have not brought her to mass. When I asked her what she means by paradise, she says "the place photographs are taken." I told her, "That's not paradise, that's Los Angeles, where we already live." Then she threw a tantrum, as if that would change things. Out in the streets, the black people were throwing a tantrum, throwing rocks into television stores and looting hospital equipment. I think she learned from them because I have never had a tantrum in her presence. I think they told her about paradise.

My daughters complain that my son has been using an
augur to blind himself.

He says he's sending a message.

To whom? He makes a picture in the air like a tower on fire.

A whore tells me she collapses the distinction between
luxury and necessity.

Los Angeles is full of collections (anemones, aquariums,
spices etc) of which my son is but one.

One day I will sell my body to the culture industry for
research on remakes of the *Merchant of Venice*.

My son won't let me be. He wants to know something
about the whores like if they would shatter windows for
him. Fashion will ruin the state, I tell him but he doesn't
understand why we are losing the war.

We are not I say but he doesn't believe me because he
has just learned how to vomit.

I don't know how he learned it, how the poisons made it
into his mouth.

So I watch a movie about Marie Antoinette.

Turn on the blowtorch.

*The Death of Sardanapalus:* In one of my favorite
performances, I watched others die while reclining in
a bed. Poised with seeming insouciance on my bed,
surrounded by riches and lushly attired, I watched the
assassination of concubines by soldiers. It's not so much
about my own death as my contemplation of death.
Death as a kind of luxury. It stages the division of my
mind against the lives of the harem's bodies. And then the
distinction collapses. The urn remains just another glowing
trinket midst the disheveled whores and their moist bodies.
It could be argued that this is an allegory of the return of
the repressed (here the political reality of the day has been
repressed in acts of erotic excess, but it then resurfaces in
that very erotic melee). It's hard for me to say. I remember
it all too well, even the sensation of velvet on my arms.

Poetry is how I buy everything: the porn and the plague
and the soldiers and the suit and the poetry and the kill
lists and the drones and the dharma and the whores
and the poetry and the rats and Korea and home and
family and chemicals and deer hearts and glue hearts and
terrorism and bombs and the mall and the empire and the
white house and the white bodies and the sugar and the
sugar bodies and the cocaine bodies and the black bodies
and the dark matter and the poetry.

I feel I'm imitating my censors.

Class hatred.

My corpse, your hatred.

I eat snails inside stadiums.

I have a fantasy about target practice.

In one mansion researchers are using rabbits to test make up.
I'm watching a film about crimes.

Don't cry, says one man. The tears might ruin the film. The
whores might ruin your make-up.

Like an idiot, I believe in cocaine socialism.

Like a nightmare I shine my shoes before the regicide.

I'm a child of Reason so I ransack the dolls.
I blame my daughters for giving my son all these ideas
like he is supposedly surrounded by snakes. Supposedly
involved in "parrot's perch."
I've read that torture book too but it was really about
beauty so why does he want to talk about escape? Why
does he act ekphrastic when he should be sleeping?
Why does he want to become famous like a murderer?
I want to solve the crime and like in sci-fi.
Let go of a drowning victim, I tell myself into a tape recorder.
Now they're exhibiting my childhood for protestors.
Now they are disinfecting meat at the shooting range.
It takes forever to transcribe this kind of party, it never ends.
Or it's the kind that ends like porn: An odd picture and an
odd sort of prisoner.
Sometimes I forget I am the Father but then
I look in the mirror
and see the white face and the rubber gloves.
Sometimes I forget to pick the splinters out of my hair.
It's disgusting to remember how they got there.

My daughters think my son wants to escape
but I think he wants to learn how to speak correctly.
He makes those ridiculous gestures with his hands
and it looks like he has the plague but he doesn't
and it looks like he wants to eat the bird in the window
and it looks like whelk in here
and he wants to be famous or he wants to destroy Los Angeles
or eradicate the vermin
it's hard to say with his hand gestures.
"I have to wake up the bleeded fox," says Majken and she
means the son.
I have refused to speak to him for several days
since he started in on the whores.
He thinks he belongs with them in Los Angeles.
I can't stop writing as if I sat on the floor surrounded by skulls.
That's funny.

My son has gone quiet in there. Perhaps he wants food.
Perhaps he is learning a new language,
in which modernity means sitting still and gaping
at that bird in the window.
Perhaps he is contemplating a story I told him about African
boys who are ghosts on account of a stolen TV.
I should never have told him about the water lilies
or the governor's virgin body. Who knows what a pure
soul like my son can make of a virgin body? Especially
considering how he falls over and crashes into the walls
and then goes quiet. I didn't tell him about the whores,
my daughters must have done that.
They must have told him about milk.
I must have told him about parties.
I'm partying on a dead girl's text. We wrote it together
like we were carving up a filmmaker's thigh. We
entertained each other like immigrants do. She would
wake up on the bathroom floor, I would wake up with
butterflies teeming on my cuts.
We both wanted a torn prom-dress for our ending.
When she died I told my son to shut up. He hasn't
spoken since.
I haven't spoken of the dead girl since the vaudeville era,
when I thought I would work as a propagandist.
Cut the decoy crap and tell them how your torso hurts.
This isn't my language. Or this is my language only if
the children are locked in a barn.

When I talked to the dead girl I talked with rabies I talked
with symbolism I talked with bathwater in my mouth.
I talked to my son about a cold war.
Maybe he is as dead as a girl. I can't stand the way he
talks now.

Moths, anomalous emperor
Moths, argent and sable
Moths, autumn gun
Moths, bag shelter
Moths, barrel egg
Moths, burner
Moths, browntail
Moths, cherry scallop shell
Moths, inflamed tigerlet
Moths, mistletoe browntail
Moths, rosey male
Moths, silver eggar
Moths, trotricid
Moths, true silk
Moths, trussock,
Moths, underwing,
Moths, wild silk

*The new austerity measures*:

To only use bullets.

To wear: Ermine Fur.

I want the snow to cover up the bodies in the street but it won't.
Sara wants the snow to fall on her pussy but it won't.
She's doing her Francesca Woodman routine but this time
with a firing squad. I'm the real Ulrike Meinhof she screams
into the camera. She looks scared.
Everybody is a threat.
This disease that invades the country is natural.
Our ears shan't be tortured with that discord and jargon.
My mother left me here three months ago.
I'm going to a party.
I'm going nowhere.
I wear white and my skin is powdered as for a photo shoot.
I've been told I'm languid.
That my heart bleeds into hers, the girl I live with. There's
a caterpillar on her shoulder and it seems to glow when she
walks to the window. The walls are covered with tapestry
and surrounded by gold frames. I'm a guest. Don't tell
me about funerals, your forms wound me. My wild heart
bleeds. I'm a guest here for three months while a plague
invades the country that surrounds us.
There is a picture I have not yet seen.
I'm asking for it.
I have a dream.
I cannot call it a nightmare.
I am asking for it.
I am perfectly myself.
See how I have recovered.

I am asking for it.
Clean the picture.
It's an effigy of me!
In the picture I have a mole and it's nature.
In the picture I have a doctor and it's a butterfly.
I have an auditory nerve with an inappropriate splendor.
Meat and vaults surround me.
I fuck nature because I am an effigy.
I'm asking for it.
I'm asking everywhere
My son is gone.
My son is gone.
It's over.

## ACKNOWLEDGEMENTS

Parts of this book have appeared in *Ampersand Review*, *Denver Quarterly*, *Fanzine*, *Iowa Review*, *Lana Turner*, *Similar Peaks*, and *The Volta*.

Texts sampled in this book include *Daniel Defoe's Journal of a Plague Year*; James P. Boyd's *Wonders of the Heavens, Earth, and Ocean as Revealed in the Starry Sky, the Vasty Deep, and all the Continents of the Globe*; Maurice Blanchot's "Two Versions of the Imaginary" and "The Gaze of Orpheus"; the last words by people killed by the Texas Department of Criminal Justice; Ann Jäderlund's Swedish translations of Emily Dickinson's poems; Lars Norén's diaries; Wikipedia; various articles and books about insects and butterflies; *Carmilla* by Joseph Sheridan Le Fanu; and many others the author can't remember.

## ABOUT THE AUTHOR

In addition to his three books with Tarpaulin Sky Press, *The Sugar Book* (2015), *Haute Surveillance* (2013) and *Entrance to a colonial pageant in which we all begin to intricate* (2011), Johannes Göransson has published three other books of his own writings—*A New Quarantine Will Take My Place*, *Dear Ra*, and *Pilot ("Johann the Carousel Horse")*. He has also translated several books, including *Dark Matter* and *With Deer* by Aase Berg, *Ideals Clearance* by Henry Parland, and *Collobert Orbital* by Johan Jönson. Together with his wife, Joyelle McSweeney, he co-edits Action Books, and with John Woods he runs *Action, Yes*, an online journal. He teaches at the University of Notre Dame in Indiana and blogs at montevidayo.com.

# TARPAULIN SKY PRESS
## Current Titles 2015

hallucinatory ... trance-inducing (*Publishers Weekly* "**Best Summer Reads**"); warped from one world to another (*The Nation*); somewhere between Artaud and Lars Von Trier (*VICE*); simultaneously metaphysical and visceral ... scary, sexual, and intellectually disarming (*Huffington Post*); only becomes more surreal (*NPR Books*); horrifying and humbling in their imaginative precision (*The Rumpus*); wholly new (*Iowa Review*); breakneck prose harnesses the throbbing pulse of language itself (*Publishers Weekly*); the opposite of boring.... an ominous conflagration devouring the bland terrain of conventional realism (*Bookslut*); creating a zone where elegance and grace can gambol with the just-plain-fucked-up (*HTML Giant*); both devastating and uncomfortably enjoyable (*American Book Review*); consistently inventive (*TriQuarterly*); playful, experimental appeal (*Publishers Weekly*); a peculiar, personal music that is at once apart from and very much surrounded by the world (*Verse*); a world of wounded voices (*Hyperallergic*); dangerous language, a murderous kind.... discomfiting, filthy, hilarious, and ecstatic (*Bookslut*); dark, multivalent, genre-bending ... unrelenting, grotesque beauty (*Publishers Weekly*); futile, sad, and beautiful (*NewPages*); refreshingly eccentric (*The Review of Contemporary Fiction*); a kind of nut job's notebook (*Publishers Weekly*); thought-provoking, inspired and unexpected. Highly recommended (*After Ellen*).

Aaron Apps's *Intersex* (2015) explores gender as it forms in concrete and unavoidable patterns in the material world. What happens when a child is born with ambiguous genitalia? What happens when a body is normalized? *Intersex* provides tangled and shifting answers to both of these questions as it questions our ideas of what is natural and normal about gender and personhood. In this hybrid-genre memoir, intersexed author Aaron Apps adopts and upends historical descriptors of hermaphroditic bodies such as "freak of nature," "hybrid," "imposter," "sexual pervert," and "unfortunate monstrosity" in order to trace his own monstrous sex as it perversely intertwines with gender expectations and medical discourse. *Intersex* leaves the reader wondering: what does it mean to be human? "*Intersex* is all feral prominence: a physical archive of the 'strange knot.' Thus: necessarily vulnerable, brave and excessive. Book as trait. Book as biology without end: modified, pulsing, visible, measured, folded then folded again: an 'animal self.' I felt this book in the middle of my own body. Like the best kind of memoir, Apps brings a reader close to an experience of life that is both 'unattainable' and attentive to 'what will emerge from things.' In doing so, he has written a book that bursts from its very frame" (BHANU KAPIL)

CLAIRE DONATO
BURIAL

The debut novella from Claire Donato that rocked the small press world. "Poetic, trance-inducing language turns a reckoning with the confusion of mortality into readerly joy at the sensuality of living." (*PUBLISHERS WEEKLY* "**BEST SUMMER READS 2013**"). "A dark, multivalent, genre-bending book.... Unrelenting, grotesque beauty an exhaustive recursive obsession about the unburiability of the dead, and the incomprehensibility of death" (*PUBLISHERS WEEKLY* **STARRED REVIEW**). "Dense, potent language captures that sense of the unreal that, for a time, pulls people in mourning to feel closer to the dead than the living.... [S]tartlingly original and effective" (*MINNEAPOLIS STAR-TRIBUNE*). "A grief-dream, an attempt to un-sew pain from experience and to reveal it in language" (*HTML GIANT*). "A full and vibrant illustration of the restless turns of a mind undergoing trauma.... Donato makes and unmakes the world with words, and what is left shimmers with pain and delight" (**Brian Evenson**). "A gorgeous fugue, an unforgettable progression, a telling I cannot shake" (**HEATHER CHRISTLE**). "Claire Donato's assured and poetic debut augurs a promising career" (**BENJAMIN MOSER**).

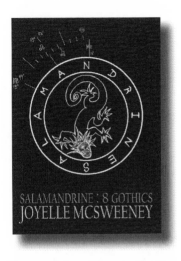

Following her debut novel from Tarpauin Sky Press, the acclaimed SPD bestseller *Nylund, The Sarcographer*, comes Joyelle McSweeney's first collection of short stories, *Salamandrine: 8 Gothics*. "Vertiginous.... Denying the reader any orienting poles for the projected reality.... McSweeney's breakneck prose harnesses the throbbing pulse of language itself" (**PUBLISHERS WEEKLY**). "Biological, morbid, fanatic, surreal, McSweeney's impulses are to go to the rhetoric of the maternity mythos by evoking the spooky, sinuous syntaxes of the gothic and the cleverly constructed political allegory. [A]t its core is the proposition that writing the mother-body is a viscid cage match with language and politics in a declining age.... [T]his collection is the sexy teleological apocrypha of motherhood literature, a siren song for those mothers 'with no soul to photograph'" (**THE BROOKLYN RAIL**). "[L]anguage commits incest with itself.... Sounds repeat, replicate, and mutate in her sentences, monstrous sentences of aural inbreeding and consangeous consonants, strung out and spinning like the dirtiest double-helix, dizzy with disease...." (**QUARTERLY WEST**).

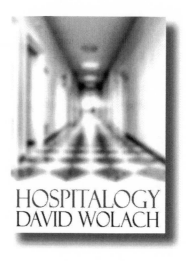

HOSPITALOGY
DAVID WOLACH

david wolach's fourth book of poetry, *Hospitalogy*, traces living forms
of intimate and militant listening within the Hospital Industrial
Complex—hospitals, medical clinics and neighboring motels—
performing a sociopoetic surgery that is exploratory, not curative.
"An extraordinary work.... [A] radical somatics, procedural anatomic
work, queer narrativity—where 'the written is explored as catastrophe
and its aftermath'" (ERICA KAUFMAN). "Dear 'distractionary quickie,'
Dear 'groundwater,' Dear 'jesus of the pain.' Welcome to david
wolach's beautiful corrosion, *Hospitalogy*" (FRED MOTEN). "At a
time when hospitality is increasingly deployed to sterilize policies of
deportation and incarceration...david wolach performs the common
detention of patients, workers, and other undesirables in 'places of
liquidation' (ELENI STECOPOULOS). "This is a book that documents
the soft rebellion of staying alive, articulating the transition from
invisibility to indecipherability" (FRANK SHERLOCK).

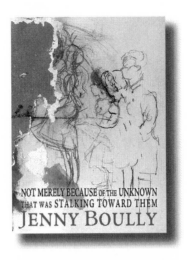

NOT MERELY BECAUSE OF THE UNKNOWN THAT WAS STALKING TOWARD THEM

JENNY BOULLY

In her second SPD bestseller from Tarpaulin Sky Press, *not merely because of the unknown that was stalking toward them*, Jenny Boully presents a "deliciously creepy" swan song from Wendy Darling to Peter Pan, as Boully reads between the lines of J. M. Barrie's *Peter and Wendy* and emerges with the darker underside, with sinister and subversive places. *not merely because of the unknown* explores, in dreamy and dark prose, how we love, how we pine away, and how we never stop loving and pining away. "This is undoubtedly the contemporary re-treatment that Peter Pan deserves.... Simultaneously metaphysical and visceral, these addresses from Wendy to Peter in lyric prose are scary, sexual, and intellectually disarming" (***Huffington Post***). "[T]o delve into Boully's work is to dive with faith from the plank — to jump, with hope and belief and a wish to see what the author has given us: a fresh, imaginative look at a tale as ageless as Peter himself" (***Bookslut***). "Jenny Boully is a deeply weird writer—in the best way" (**Ander Monson**).

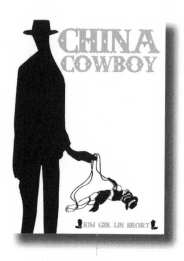

Kim Gek Lin Short's searing second novel from Tarpaulin Sky, *China Cowboy*, unfolds in a technicolor timewarp called Hell, Hong Kong, where wannabe cowgirl La La is hellbent on realizing her dream to be a folk-singing sensation—alive or dead. "Short is an elegant, entrancing writer. [*China Cowboy*] is both devastating and uncomfortably enjoyable" (*AMERICAN BOOK REVIEW*). "A satanically intricate narrative with seemingly infinite vantage points in space, time and sympathy ... has expanded and fused the poetic and narrative fields, creating a zone where elegance and grace can gambol with the just-plain-fucked-up" (*HTML GIANT*). "Grossly disturbing and excruciatingly seductive, catching the reader in a tense push and pull with and against the text.... Short binds us within tales of fierce femme survival" (*LANTERN REVIEW*). "[A]s savage as it is entertaining, [*China Cowboy*]—while bleak—is a marvel of modern storytelling, [with] characters whose stories will haunt you long after you finish the book, and will more than likely draw you back for another read" (*COLDFRONT MAGAZINE'S TOP 40 POETRY BOOKS OF 2012*).

**FABLES**
Sarah Goldstein

Departing from the Brothers Grimm to approach our own economically and socially fractured present, Sarah Goldstein's fiction/prose-poetry debut, *Fables*, constructs a world defined by small betrayals, transformations, and brutality amid its animal and human inhabitants. "Goldstein's vision and approach is wholly new. Her work in this collection is more than translation and transcription: *Fables* contains poems that whisper tradition but fully stand on their own" (***The Iowa Review***) "Horrifying and humbling in their imaginative precision, the stories ... awaken the tension between human and nonhuman in these haunting vignettes.... [B]e sure not to leave this one laying out for the kids" (***The Rumpus***). "A gorgeous intertwining of allegorical stories presented in tiny fragments, dare I say breadcrumbs!, that display a horrifying yet beautiful world where mayors keep bones in boxes and ghosts enter through the beaks of birds" (***Specter Magazine***). "In the meadow of fairy tale, Goldstein unrolls ribbons of story that fly gamely and snap with brilliance. Truly worth gazing at" (**Deb Olin Unferth**).

# SELECT BACKLIST

## CHAPBOOKS

&

## Tarpaulin Sky Literary Journal
*in print and online*

# TARPAULINSKY.COM